this journal belongs to

_____

date I started this study

_____

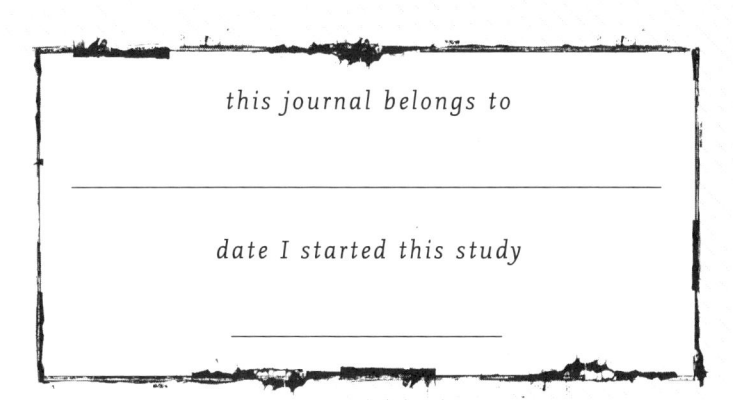

COVENANT
KNOWING GOD
HIS RELATIONSHIP WITH HIS PEOPLE

COVENANT
KNOWING GOD
HIS RELATIONSHIP WITH HIS PEOPLE

By Dr. David Platt

Clarity Publishers
Birmingham, AL

Clarity Publishers
P.O. Box 361726
Birmingham, AL 35236

To order additional copies of this resource, call the publisher at 888.811.9934
or order online at www.studentlifebiblestudy.com.

Inside images © jupiterimages, BananaStock, Comstock, and Photodisc.

Table of **Contents**

Editorial and Design **Staff**

Executive Editor
Andy Blanks

Associate Editor
Lynn Waldrep

Copy Editor
Libby Minor

Graphic Design
Brandi K. Etheredge

Vice President, Ministry Resources
Paul Kelly

Author

David Platt—David Platt is originally from Stone Mountain, Georgia, and now lives in New Orleans, Louisiana, with his wife, Heather. As a professor at New Orleans Baptist Theological Seminary, David teaches how to communicate God's Word and defend one's faith. He is also on staff at Edgewater Baptist Church, where he's responsible for coordinating inner-city ministries to the homeless, internationals, and college students.

But that's not where it stops. David preaches throughout North America and is extensively involved in traveling to other nations. At any time during the year, you could find him crossing a crocodile-infested river in Africa, helping build churches in Central America, telling people about Jesus in India, or training underground church leaders in countries where it's illegal to follow Christ. Whether he's sleeping in a mud hut or watching his wife eat duck feet and pig ear, David enjoys the journey of making disciples in all nations.

David graduated from the University of Georgia with degrees in journalism and speech communication, and from New Orleans Baptist Theological Seminary with a Master's in Divinity, Master's in Theology, and Ph.D. in Preaching. He also began WhyNot Ministries, a nonprofit organization aimed at mobilizing God's people to experience God's global purpose for their lives. You can find more information on David's ministry at www.whynotministries.net.

Essential Truths

As Christians, there are some essential truths we believe. We discover these truths in the Bible. At Student Life, we have identified eight truths we believe are essential for every Christian to know and understand. These statements are descriptions of those biblical truths and have been developed to help you talk about your faith. They will help you know what you believe.

GOD IS
Only one true and living God exists. He is the Creator of the universe, eternally existing in three Persons-the Father, Son, and Holy Spirit-each equally deserving of humanity's worship and obedience. He is infinite and perfect in all His attributes.

THE BIBLE IS GOD'S WORD
The Bible is God's written revelation to people, divinely given through human authors who were inspired by the Holy Spirit. It is entirely true. The Bible is totally sufficient and completely authoritative for matters of life and faith. The goal of God's Word is the restoration of humanity into His image.

PEOPLE ARE GOD'S TREASURE
God created people in His image for His glory. They are the crowning work of His creation. Yet every person has willfully disobeyed God-an act known as sin-thus inheriting both physical and spiritual death and the need for salvation. All human beings are born with a sin-nature and into an environment inclined toward sin. Only by the grace of God through Jesus Christ can they experience salvation.

JESUS IS GOD AND SAVIOR
Jesus is both fully God and fully human. He is Christ, the Son of God. Born of a virgin, He lived a sinless life and performed many miracles. He died on the cross to provide people forgiveness of sin and eternal salvation. Jesus rose from the dead, ascended to the right hand of the Father, and will return in power and glory.

THE HOLY SPIRIT IS GOD AND EMPOWERER
The Holy Spirit is supernatural and sovereign, baptizing all believers into the Body of Christ. He lives within every Christian beginning at the moment of salvation and then empowers them for bold witness and effective service as they yield to Him. The Holy Spirit convicts individuals of sin, uses God's Word to mature believers into Christ-likeness, and secures them until Christ returns.

SALVATION IS BY FAITH ALONE
All human beings are born with a sin nature, separated from God, and in need of a Savior. That salvation comes only through a faith relationship with Jesus Christ, the Savior, as a person repents of sin and receives Christ's forgiveness and eternal life. Salvation is instantaneous and accomplished solely by the power of the Holy Spirit through the Word of God. This salvation is wholly of God by grace on the basis of the shed blood of Jesus Christ and not on the basis of human works. All the redeemed are secure in Christ forever.

THE CHURCH IS GOD'S PLAN
The Holy Spirit immediately places all people who put their faith in Jesus Christ into one united spiritual body, the Church, of which Christ is the head. The primary expression of the Church on earth is in autonomous local congregations of baptized believers. The purpose of the Church is to glorify God by taking the gospel to the entire world and by building its members up in Christ-likeness through the instruction of God's Word, fellowship, service, worship, and prayer.

THE FUTURE IS IN GOD'S HANDS
God will bring the world to its appropriate end in His own time and in His own way. At that time, Jesus Christ will return personally and visibly in glory to the earth. Both the saved and unsaved will be resurrected physically to be judged by Christ. Those who have trusted Christ will receive their reward and dwell forever in heaven with the Lord. Those who have refused Christ will spend eternity in hell, the place of everlasting punishment. The certain return of Christ motivates believers to be faithful in their daily lives.

How To This Book

The purpose of this 48-week journal is to help you learn the story of God's covenant with His people. Though the stories contained in this journal span thousands of years, they are relevant today. You can still apply the biblical truths of those stories to your life as a 21st century Christian living under God's covenant. Through this journal, you will learn how God longs to be in relationship with us and how He has provided for such a relationship to exist. This journal includes a few different sections each week to help you as you learn. Here's how to use them.

Introductions

These are short sections introducing each week of devotions. If you are studying the COVENANT series on Sunday mornings, Wednesday nights, or in small groups, each week of devotions will coincide with what you are studying in class. Read the introductions to get a picture of what the week's devotions will center on.

Daily Devotions

Now we're getting to the good stuff! The journal is designed to walk you through five days of devotions per week. Each devotion has Scripture passages and a few para-graphs of text. Always start by reading the Scripture passages from your Bible, and then read the text. Look for ways in which the text unlocks truths of Scripture you may not have noticed before.

Daily Questions

After each devotion, there are questions designed to get you thinking. When you read these questions, take a moment to really think about what they are asking. Listen to the Holy Spirit as He teaches you through Scripture. Then record your thoughts in the journal space.

Journal Space

You will notice this book is different from many books you have read before. It is designed to be filled with your thoughts. Use the space provided to record your reactions to each devotion. Or use it to write a prayer request or praise to God. Use it any way you please. It's your journal! There are no rules, just guidelines. The important thing is to listen to the Lord and open your heart in response to His leading.

If you take the time to read the devotions prayerfully and with the anticipation that God will reveal new things to you, you will be amazed at what will flow through your pen or pencil onto the pages.

Introduction

When I think about covenant, I think about my first date. I sat nervously next to this beautiful girl and wondered what to do. I asked myself, "Should I try to hold her hand? How will she respond if I do?" I'd never been on a date before, and I was clueless about how to act! So I mustered up the courage and casually slipped my hand next to hers. And then . . . she reached back! And that's how my relationship with my wife began. I'm thankful she held my hand that first night, and I'm thankful she decided to keep holding it after that!

A covenant is a relationship between two people. It's what happens when two people make an unchanging commitment to one another. When my wife and I began a relationship with each other, when we committed ourselves to each other, we entered into a covenant. That covenant now affects my life every day. But what's even cooler is that you and I have the privilege of entering into a covenant with God. Similar to the way I reached out my hand to my wife on our first date, the God of the universe has reached out His hand to you and me! He has initiated a relationship with us and we have the incredible honor of committing our lives to Him. That's what a covenant is all about.

This year, we have the opportunity to take a look at what it means to be in covenant with God. This is one of the most incredible themes of the Bible, but it is often overlooked. Unfortunately, when most of us hear the word covenant, we really don't know what to think. It doesn't really sound that incredible. You might even be thinking, "Is it really worth spending almost a year looking at the meaning of covenant?" I believe it is. The idea of God's covenant has huge significance for our lives, both now and for eternity.

As we begin to study and reflect on God's covenant with us, I want us to think about four characteristics of covenant in the Bible. We will refer to these cthroughout this journal as we study Scripture, write notes, and spend time in prayer discovering what covenant means.

First, the Bible uses covenant to describe God's relationship with us. We don't have a God who is way up in heaven separated from what goes on in our lives every day. Instead, God has passionately pursued a relationship with us and He is personally involved in every detail of our lives. Whether we are at home or at school, with family or with friends, playing sports or listening to music, God is there. And the Bible uses covenant to describe the way God relates to us.

Second, covenant describes God's unchanging promises to His people. When I was married and entered into a covenant relationship with my wife, I made a promise that I would be with her for the rest of my life. Unfortunately, many times in our society, these types of promises get broken, and so we begin to think God may not keep His promises. But the more we study covenant in the Bible, the more we will see that God never lets His people down. In all of history, He has never made a promise that He did not keep. He is not planning on changing anytime soon!

Third, God's covenant with His people is built completely on His grace. We will see the importance of grace in God's covenant with us throughout the year, but for now it is best for us to simply realize that we are able to enter into a covenant with God because He loved us first. We cannot earn our way into a relationship with God. We cannot impress Him with all of the good things we do. Our efforts are not the foundation for a covenant with God. Instead, the foundation for covenant is grace. We have the opportunity to be in covenant with God not because of who we are or because of what we've done, but because of who He is and because of what He has done.

Finally, we are able to enter into a covenant with God only by faith. Faith involves us simply believing that what God says in His Word is true. That's why it's important for us to study covenant in Scripture. We need to know what the unchanging promises of God are before we can believe in them. Then, when we believe in His promises, faith involves trusting Him with our lives. And this is where covenant

really starts to affect us every day. The more we understand God's covenant with us, the more we trust Him with our families, our friendships, our plans, our dreams, and our futures. When we trust Him with our lives, we start to realize how trustworthy He really is!

So imagine the picture: God has reached out His hand, passionately pursuing a relationship with you. And you reach back. You enter into a relationship with the God of the universe. What does this relationship mean for your life now?

Well, turn the page, and let the journey begin.

Why A Covenant?

memory verse

This is the covenant I will make with the house of Israel after that time, declares the Lord. I will put my laws in their minds and write them on their hearts. I will be their God, and they will be my people.

Hebrews 8:10

Imagine your closest friends. How is this bond of friendship created? Maybe it's by hanging out, communicating via email or IM, or talking on the phone. Maybe it's through common interests you have. Whatever the reason, the more you spend time with those people, the more you bond with them.

The word "covenant" in the Bible can also mean "bond." God's covenant with us describes how we bond with Him. Now, you may be wondering, "How do I bond with God?" That's a good question. Ever since the beginning of creation, God has been bonding with His people through covenants. He makes promises to His people, and these promises are the foundations for His relationships with them.

This week we'll look at God's covenant with us. We'll see how God bonded with His people in the Old Testament. We'll see how God's people disobeyed Him, breaking their covenant. But thankfully that's not where the Bible ends. We're going to see how God established a new covenant with His people.

Our covenant with God defines how He relates to us and we relate to Him. So let's check out what a covenant is and see how God's new covenant affects the way we bond with Him.

covenant: Knowing God—His Relationship With His People

Day 1 >

**Hebrews 8:8-12;
Jeremiah 31:31-34**

Let's compare these two passages of Scripture. Why are they so similar? The author of Hebrews is quoting from a passage in Jeremiah. Look at both passages and count the number of times the phrase "declares the Lord" is repeated. Why is this important? Because God declares the terms of the covenant, not us.

Our job is obedience. We are to listen to God's Word so that we know exactly what He wants us to do. Then we do it. We're not in a position to dictate to God what we will do or to bargain with God. The wild thing is the more we get to know God, the more we realize we can trust Him. And the more we trust Him, the more we will want to obey Him.

Have you ever been tempted to tell God what you think is best for your life instead of trusting Him to show you what is best? What did you learn about trusting God's Word during that time? Write a prayer asking God to help you to obey Him no matter what He tells you to do.

Day 2 >>

Hebrews 8:9; Exodus 20:1-21

What did the covenant God had with the Israelites look like? Read Exodus 20:1-21.

This passage shows us how God gave the Ten Commandments to His people. These were the basic rules that governed the Israelites' part of the covenant. But the people were unable to keep God's commands. A new covenant was needed.

A covenant relationship with God has some awesome benefits. It also includes. responsibility. It's the same way in all of our relationships. Think about your closest friend. You enjoy having that person in your life, but you also have a responsibility to be loyal and to build up the relationship.

Write down three benefits of being in covenant with God. Then list three responsibilities we have in our covenant with God. Say a prayer to God asking Him to help you fulfill those responsibilities.

Day 3 >>>

Hebrews 8:10; Ezekiel 36:24-28

Yesterday, we read how the Israelites failed to keep God's covenant. But in spite of how the Israelites disobeyed God, He made a new covenant with them. Isn't it good to know that God never fails us?

In Hebrews 8:10, God said He would write His covenant on the Israelites' hearts. God said a similar thing in Ezekiel 36:24-28. He promised to give His people a new heart. This is huge in our understanding of covenant.

We're like the Israelites, aren't we? We think we can just do better next time. We get up, dust ourselves off, and try again. But we find ourselves failing. We need the transformed heart God promises, a heart filled with His Spirit. That's the only way we are ever going to walk in covenant with Him.

Write a prayer to God thanking Him that he has given you a new heart. Thank Him for filling you with His Spirit. As you think about having God's Word written on your heart, spend some time memorizing this week's memory verse—Hebrews 8:10.

Day 4 >>>>

Hebrews 8:11; Hebrews 4:14-16

Hebrews 8:11 is not saying we don't need people to teach us the Bible. It's saying we all have the opportunity to know God. This is important because many people in the world today still think they need to go through another person to have access to God.

Read Hebrews 4:14-16. Everyone can enter into the presence of God. This is not a privilege for a few; through Jesus, each of us has access to God! What does this mean to you? A lot, actually. It means you can know God personally. You can talk to Him, rely on Him, and learn why He is the way He is. More than that, you have access to the power of His Spirit that lives within you. Take a few minutes to write how your life is different because you have a personal knowledge of God.

Day 5 >>>>>
Hebrews 8:12-13; Psalm 103:8-18

What makes the new covenant "new"? Easy. The forgiveness of sins. We've talked about how God never breaks His covenant. Just because there's a new covenant, that doesn't mean the old covenant wasn't good or that God didn't keep it.

Let me explain. God's purpose in the old covenant was to have a relationship with His children, but sin kept that from happening. So God planned the ultimate provision: Jesus. His death and resurrection conquered sin once and for all. It's only because of Jesus' death that we have the unbelievable privilege of "bonding" with God today.

As we close this week, spend some time confessing areas of your life where you have broken your covenant with God. Write a song, poem, or prayer of thanks to God for the forgiveness you have through Christ. Finish by reading Psalm 103:8-18 as a prayer of praise to God.

Old Covenant and New Covenant

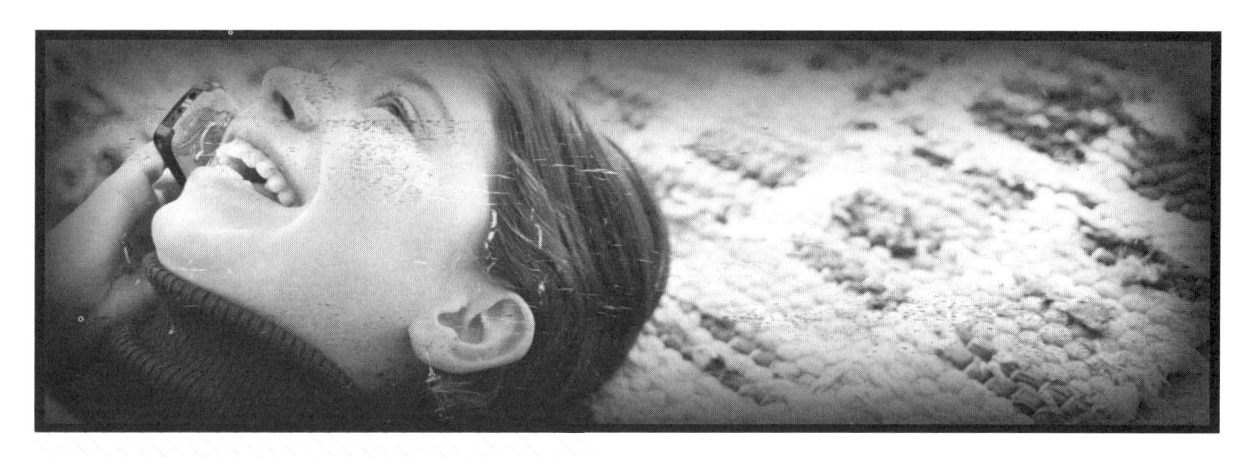

memory verse

Before this faith came, we were held prisoners by the law, locked up until faith should be revealed. So the law was put in charge to lead us to Christ that we might be justified by faith. **Galatians 3:23-24**

Key lime pie is my favorite dessert. When my wife and I were dating, she decided to surprise me. She arrived at my house one night with a homemade Key lime pie. I was so excited. I couldn't wait to eat it! The only problem was that my soon-to-be wife had accidentally left out a key ingredient from the pie. She had done everything right except for this one thing. And we both agreed that it didn't quite taste like a normal Key lime pie!

Remember our talk last week about the old covenant and new covenant? The old covenant wasn't bad. It clearly demonstrated God's love and favor for His people. But just like my wife's Key lime pie, the old covenant was missing a key ingredient.

The components of the old covenant included obedience to God's Law and complete devotion to His Word. There was a problem, though; the Israelites couldn't live up to the standards of God's Law. What they needed was the key ingredient: Jesus Christ.

When Jesus came to the earth, He completed what the Old Testament had started. He was fully obedient to the Law of God. He paid the price for our disobedience. As a result, we can be saved by simply putting our faith in Jesus.

This week, let's check out Galatians 3:19-25 so we can understand this more.

Day 1 >

Galatians 3:19-20;
Deuteronomy 4:5-14

In Galatians 3, the Apostle Paul tells us why God gave us His Law. In Deuteronomy 4:5-14 we see that God wanted the Israelites to be wise so that all the other nations would be amazed. Then those nations would see how much God loved His children. The other nations would then want to serve God as well.

God spoke to the Israelites in an audible voice. He speaks to us today, but in a different way. We have the Bible, God's Word. Sometimes we forget what a privilege this is. I have worked with Christians around the world who don't have access to Bibles. Whenever they get a chance to read or even touch a page from one, their eyes light up with excitement. God's Word is extremely important in His covenant relationship with His people.

Do you have favorite verses? Write down some of them. If you want, note why these verses mean so much to you.

Day 2 >>

Galatians 3:21; Romans 3:9-20

We all stand silent before God because we have all sinned. According to Paul, the Law's purpose was to reveal that we cannot live up to the standard of righteousness on our own.

covenant: Knowing God—His Relationship With His People

Some of you may be thinking, "I thought God gave the Law out of love! Why would He give us the Law if it were only going to condemn us?" That's pretty much the same question Paul asked in Galatians 3:21. His response was that the Law does, indeed, show us where we fall short. But it also shows us our need for a Savior, whom God has provided in Jesus.

Do you remember the events surrounding your decision to accept Christ as your Savior? Record some of the emotions or thoughts that come to mind when you recall this moment.

Day 3

Galatians 3:21-22; Romans 3:21-31

The Bible teaches that we are all sinners before our Creator. Maybe the most important question we can ask is, "How can we be saved from our sins?" Galatians 3:21-22 answers this question.

The Jews thought they could be made right before God by obeying the Law. If they did enough good things, maybe they would be OK. But look at what Paul says in Romans 3:21-31. No one can be saved from their sins by being a good person or doing great things for God.

The only way we can be made right before God is by our faith in Jesus Christ through God's grace. Does this mean that we don't obey God or do great things for Him? Absolutely not. But instead of doing these things in order to earn salvation, we obey God because He has already saved us.

Write out a few specific ways you can obey God today—not to earn His favor but as a result of the love you have for Him and the desire to obey the Father. Then, ask God for strength to obey Him in these ways.

Day 4 >>>>>

Galatians 3:23-24; John 14:1-7

Many people believe there are different paths to God and they can choose whichever one works best for them. It's as if God were at the top of a mountain. One person may climb one path while another takes a different route. In the end, they would both finish at the same place.

This mountain analogy sounds clever. But what if God decided to come down the mountain? Would it make a difference? Of course it would. Well, that's exactly what God did! He came down to us in the person of Jesus because we could not have made our own way to Him.

Read Galatians 3:23-24. Now read John 14:1-7. We can take heart knowing that Jesus has already made the path for us. Do you know someone who doesn't know the truth about Jesus? Write this person's initials. Then write what you would say if you were to tell that person about Jesus.

Day 5 >>>>>

Galatians 3:25-26; 2 Corinthians 5:16-21

As we near the end of Galatians 3, Paul sums up the difference between the old covenant and the new covenant. The Law was emphasized in the old covenant, but the people of God could never fully obey it. The new covenant completes the old covenant by emphasizing faith in Jesus.

In 2 Corinthians 5:16-21, Paul talks about how, for Christians, the old has gone and the new has come. Through our faith in Jesus, we've been freed from our failure to obey God's Law. Now we are free to relate to Him in the new covenant. The key ingredient has come, and our salvation is complete simply by your belief in Jesus.

Thank God today for the freedom we have through the new covenant. Write down one way you can draw closer to Jesus today.

The Righteousness of Christ

I have been crucified with Christ and I no longer live, but Christ lives in me. The life I live in the body, I live by faith in the Son of God, who loved me and gave himself for me. **Galatians 2:20**

People around the world have different ideas about salvation. Muslims follow five particular rules, or "pillars," they believe a person is saved if he or she does more good than bad. Buddhists believe that if they follow a certain path to avoid suffering in this life, they will achieve salvation in a state of paradise. Hindus believe in reincarnation, in which they supposedly have many different lives, with their next life dependent on how well they live this one.

What is similar about these views? In each one you must do certain things to earn your way to God. Remember the question we looked at last week? "How can we be saved from our sins?" No matter how many good things I might do, I still sin, right? As a result, none of the religions mentioned above really answer the question, because none of these paths helps us to get rid of sin in our lives. So how can we be saved?

The revolutionary teaching of Christianity is that there is nothing you can "do" to earn salvation. Instead, salvation comes only in what has been "done" for you. This week, we are going to learn that we can only be made right before God through what has already been done for us in the life, death, and resurrection of Christ. And in the process, we're going to see what makes Christianity unique among all the religions of the world.

Day 1

Galatians 2:15-16; Romans 4:13-25

Some people believe they can earn salvation by going to church and "doing right." Read Galatians 2:15-16 and Romans 4:13-25. Here, Paul is pretty clear: Acting right won't save us. We are saved by faith alone—faith in Jesus, that is. This week, we are going to look at the foundation of our salvation: our faith.

Write down some thoughts about faith. What is faith? How real is your faith? Ask God to increase your faith this week as you study His Word.

Day 2

Galatians 2:17-19; Ephesians 2:8-10

If salvation is by faith alone, does that mean Christians can live their lives however they want? That's the question Paul answered in Galatians 2:17-19. Paul said no one who is freed from the Law by faith will continue to live the way they used to live. In Ephesians 2:8-9 he said that we are saved by faith alone. The result of our faith (according to Eph. 2:10) is evident in our actions.

Once someone places his or her faith in Christ, good works that honor God will be the natural result. It's like a math equation. Many people believe:

FAITH + WORKS = SALVATION.

So they try to work in order to be saved. But the Bible is teaching us a different equation. God is saying that

$$FAITH = SALVATION + WORKS.$$

To put it differently, we are saved by faith alone but not by a faith that is alone.

How has your relationship with Jesus changed the way you live your life? Make a list of the "works" that should naturally result from your salvation.

Day 3 >>>
Galatians 2:20;
2 Corinthians 5:21

Have you noticed the underlying tension in what we've been discussing? We've learned that our salvation is not decided by whether or not we do good things. Instead, we are saved by believing in Jesus. But we also know that we are still supposed to do good things; we're supposed to be righteous. Yet we are to be righteous out of obedience, not to earn God's approval. Feel the tension?

How can we be righteous when we are sinful? Galatians 2:20 sheds light on this. Our sinful natures were crucified with Christ. If we have accepted Jesus as our Savior, He lives in us through the Holy Spirit. Now, look at 2 Corinthians 5:21. Sinless Jesus took our place so we could take on His righteousness. In a sense, we are righteous because Jesus was righteous. We do good because we have the righteousness of Christ inside of us.

How would you describe God's love for you? Write how you have witnessed God's love for you in your life.

Day 4 >>>>

Galatians 2:20; 2 Corinthians 5:21

I remember when I was about to get married. I was still in college, but my wife had already graduated and gotten a job. While I was making no money, she was making a salary. Now, on the day we got married, I received many wonderful gifts, the most important one being my beautiful wife. But do you know what else I received? A full bank account!

In a much greater way, this is what happens when we place our faith in the righteousness of Christ. Paul stated in 2 Corinthians 5:21 that God took all that was in Christ's account and deposited it in us.

Think about what this means! You and I can stand before a holy God, not because of how good we are or because of all that we have done, but because we have the righteousness of Christ in us!

Spend some time today journaling about how the righteousness of Christ living in you should affect the way you live every day.

Day 5 >>>>>

Galatians 2:21; Luke 9:23-27

By what means do we gain righteousness? What jump-started the holy deposit into our spiritual bank account? One word: grace. Paul says in Galatians 2:21 that this is not to be "set aside." Without grace, we would never have received the gift of Jesus Christ. None of us could do enough to earn what Jesus did for us.

Jesus told his disciples they would need to take up their crosses and follow Him (Luke 9:23). Jesus' disciples followed His example, most of them ultimately dying for the Gospel. And many people around the world are doing the same thing today—losing their lives for the One who loved them and gave Himself for them.

Take time to memorize Galatians 2:20 this week. In fact, write it down a couple of times to help you learn it. As you do, think about what it means to be crucified with Christ. How can you live today by faith in the Son of God, who loves you and gave Himself for you?

covenant: Knowing God—His Relationship With His People

God's Creative Intention

So God created man in his own image, in the image of God he created him; male and female he created them.

Genesis 1:27

Have you ever thought about why God created us? Genesis 1:26 says, "Then God said, 'Let us make man in our image, in our likeness, and let them rule over the fish of the sea and the birds of the air, over the livestock, over all the earth, and over all the creatures that move along the ground..'"

"Our likeness?" Wasn't it just God? Scripture tells us that not only does God the Father exist, but Jesus is also God (John 1:1-14; 8:58; 10:30). In addition, the Holy Spirit is God (Acts 5:3-4; Ps. 139:7-8; 1 Cor. 2:10-11). The Father is God, the Son is God, and the Spirit is God. There is one God who exists in three persons. This is called the Trinity. Hard to grasp? The Bible teaches that we cannot comprehend the greatness of God.

Covenant is all about how God relates to us as His people. God is a relational God. That is why He has created us—for a relationship with Him. And He didn't simply drop humanity into a cool little garden and call it a day. No, He placed His creation in the perfect environment. Adam and Eve had everything they could ever ask for. But Adam and Eve's sin threw everything off balance. Intrigued? Let's go on a journey this week to understand what this means.

Day 1 >

Genesis 1:1-27; Matthew 6:25-34

God created humankind so He could personally relate to us. In Genesis 1, you'll notice that often, when God created something, He said, "Let there be . . ." But in Genesis 1:26 when God created man He used a much more personal tone: "Let us make . . ." From the very beginning of time, God has intended to have a personal relationship with His people. It's the same relationship Jesus talked about when he described God's love for His people.

Read Matthew 6:25-34, and think about the many ways God cares for you. Sometimes we are tempted to view God as a detached being who does not relate to us. But this is not what covenant is all about. From our creation, God has shown us that He desires a relationship with us.

Look back at Matthew 6:25-26. Write some of the needs God meets in your life. Then write a prayer thanking Him for His love and care for you.

Day 2 >>

Genesis 1:21-27; Colossians 3:1-11

In order for God to relate to us personally, He has created us in His image. This quality sets us apart from every other living creature on earth. In Genesis 1:21, 24, and 25, the other creatures were created "according to their kinds." But in Genesis 1:27, man was created according to the image of God. This is an incredible thought . . . made in the image of God!

Now, this doesn't mean that we are equal with God or even that we look exactly like God. But it does mean that among all the creatures of the earth, we are the only ones who reflect His likeness. In the same way, we are created to reflect the likeness of God to the rest of creation. Read Colossians 3:1-11. Here, Paul talks about the importance of reflecting God's image.

Write down some areas of your life that reflect the likeness of God. What parts of your life are not reflecting his image?

Day 3 >>>
Genesis 1:26-27; Psalm 139

A lot of people talk about having a good self-image. "You should always feel good about yourself," they tell us. "Think positively, and you will have a healthy self-image." Well, the Bible actually tells us something a little different.

The key is not to focus on self but to focus on God in us. God created us, from our personalities to our bodies. Many times, we are frustrated by the way we look, the way we feel, or even the way we act. But remember God made us in His image. We literally have Him in us.

Which is more important: a healthy self-image or a healthy God-image? Write down what you think is the difference between the two? Read Psalm 139 out loud. Let this be a prayer to God as you reflect on the unique way He has created you.

Day 4 >>>>>
Genesis 1:26-27; Psalm 8:1-9

Have you ever taken care of someone? What did that involve? Genesis 1:26 says that we were created with special authority on earth. God has given us the authority to rule over the rest of creation. Look at Psalm 8:1-9 for an even greater picture of our authority in God's creation.

What does it mean to rule with God over His creation? God rules with justice, with mercy, with love, and with grace. He does not take sin lightly, but at the same time He is compassionate. These are the ways you and I are supposed to rule in creation. We have the responsibility to show God's justice, His mercy, His love, His grace, His attitude toward sin, and His compassion to all of creation.

You have been created with a certain responsibility. How can you show these characteristics of God with the authority He has given you?

Day 5 >>>>>

Genesis 1:28; Psalm 67

What do you think of when you hear the word "bless"? Maybe you picture something good that happens to someone as a "blessing." Maybe you imagine receiving a gift as a "blessing." Maybe the first thing you think about is hearing someone sneeze and saying, "God bless you"!

From the very beginning of creation, God blessed His people. His blessings always involve a promise and a purpose. In Genesis 1:28, God promised to make them be fruitful and multiply for the purpose of ruling over His creation. Read Psalm 67. In verse 1 we see a prayer that God would bless His people with love and favor. In verse 2 we see the purpose—so that God's ways and salvation might be known in all nations. When we think about covenant, we think about God's blessings for God's purposes.

Make a list of some of the blessings in your life. Then, beside each blessing, write down the purpose of each blessing. Pray that God will help you to use His blessings for His purposes.

Adam's Work

memory verse

The Lord formed the man from the dust of the ground and breathed into his nostrils the breath of life, and the man became a living being. **Genesis 2:7**

What is your family situation like? Are your parents married? Divorced? Do you live with both your parents? Just one? Or do you live with a relative or guardian? Whatever your situation, it's safe to say that someone makes sure you have a roof over your head and food on the table. (And, if you're lucky, a nice car in the driveway, an Xbox 360, and cool clothes.) In other words, they provide for you.

What do you have to do to earn this provision? To justify letting you sleep in a bedroom instead of on the streets? To prove that you are worthy to be given food to eat instead of having to provide your own? In most cases, you don't have to do much (except maybe some chores here and there). Your parents or guardian provide for you out of love. And you could boil down your end of the bargain to one simple word: obedience. Ultimately, your parents desire your love, respect, and obedience.

God's covenant relationship with us is like that. Genesis 2 describes what God's covenant with us was designed to look like. God provided everything for His creation, and He commanded Adam to obey Him so that he would continue to experience all that was designed for him. What's our part? Let's take a look at Genesis 2:7-17 this week to see what our relationship with God was designed to be like.

Day 1 >

Genesis 2:7-9; Genesis 5:21-24

God put His most treasured creation in the Garden of Eden. In this land God provided for everything man needed so that man could walk with Him and fully delight in His presence.

God's provision is one of the basic foundations of our covenant relationship with Him. God provides so that we can walk with and enjoy Him. Read Genesis 5:21-24. These verses tell us about Enoch. We don't know a lot about him, but the Bible tells us "Enoch walked with God." That's the only description we have of him. Great way to be remembered, huh? Wouldn't it be awesome if the description of your life was simply that you walked with God?

In your own words, what does it mean to walk with God? Write a description of what that looks like. Focus today on walking with God, enjoying His presence and all that He provides for you.

Day 2 >>

Genesis 2:10-14; Revelation 22:1-5

High in the Andes Mountains, the sun hits the face of an ice-clad rock, and a little gurgle of water begins to flow. As it progresses, it forms little rivulets of water, joining other rivulets of water until they become little streams. Then, almost 4,000 miles later, the Amazon River flows into the Atlantic.

Read Genesis 2:10-14. The Garden of Eden was full of beautiful rivers. Now read what Revelation 22:1-5 says about heaven. This is similar to the description of the garden. Now, we don't know exactly what the garden looked like. And we don't know what heaven will look like. But based on the descriptions we get in the Bible, we will be spending eternity in a beauty that words can barely describe.

Spend time thanking God for the beauty awaiting us when we join Him in heaven one day. How should your anticipation of heaven affect the way you live today?

Day 3 >>>
Genesis 2:10-14;
Revelation 21:1-7

Weddings are quite a spectacle, aren't they? Extravagant decorations, nicely dressed people, lots of great food. I remember the day I was married. You know, it really didn't matter to me how good the flowers looked, what everyone was wearing, or how great the food was. The only thing that mattered to me was that my wife was there!

Everything in the garden was perfect simply because God was there. Read

Revelation 21:1-7, which is another description of heaven. You will notice once again the almost indescribable beauty of that scene. The Bible emphasizes that finally God and man will enjoy each other's presence completely.

How do you see the beauty of God's presence today? Record some of the ways God is present in the world around you.

Day 4 >>>>

Genesis 2:15; Isaiah 43:1-7

Why was man put in the Garden of Eden? Some Bible translations say man was in the garden "to work it and take care of it." Last week in Genesis 1 we learned that God commanded man to rule over the earth. Man's care for the garden was a reflection of his obedience to God.

We have already seen that God provided completely for man in the garden. But that is only half of what covenant is about. In man's relationship with God, we take all that He gives us and then we worship Him by obeying His commands. This is what a relationship with God is all about.

Read Isaiah 43:1-7. This is an example of this kind of relationship. Notice in verse 7 that God tells His people that He created them for His glory. We were created to worship God with all that He gives us. Make a list of some of the things God has provided for you. Then, reflect on how you can worship God with what He has given you. Write your thoughts.

Day 5 >>>>>>

Genesis 2:16-17; Deuteronomy 30:1-10

In verses 16-17, God gave man a command: Do not eat from the tree. God said that if man disobeyed Him, he would be cut off from the delight of God's presence. If man obeyed God, he would enjoy God's perfect provision. But if he disobeyed God, he would die. In other words, he would be separated from a perfect relationship with God. Read Deuteronomy 30:1-10. God said the same thing to His people many years later.

The Bible teaches us that our delight in this life is dependent on our obedience to God's commands. When we follow His Word, we experience eternal joy. But when we disobey Him, we experience the opposite, and we miss out on the beauty of our relationship with God.

As we close this week, spend some time journaling about the joy you find in your obedience to God and the pain you experience because of your disobedience. Think about what it is going to be like when we spend eternity with Him, enjoying His presence forever.

The Fall

"You will not surely die," the serpent said to the woman. "For God knows that when you eat of it your eyes will be opened, and you will be like God, knowing good and evil." **Genesis 3:4-5**

In 1992, Derek Redmond was representing Great Britain in the Barcelona Olympics. It had come down to one race to see who would go to the finals. The race started, and Redmond was off! He was running one of his best races ever. But as he rounded a turn, he suddenly tore a muscle and fell to the track. Derek Redmond sat alone in his lane, overcome with pain, his hopes of winning a medal gone.

Redmond's story is a lot like the story of humankind. God created Adam and Eve and placed them in the Garden of Eden. Everything was going well. But something happened that caused them to fall. Satan tempted Eve to try fruit from the tree of the knowledge of good and evil. This wouldn't have been so terrible if this weren't the only thing God had ordered Adam and Eve not to do. But Eve gave in to temptation and ate. And she gave the fruit to Adam, and he ate as well. The rest is history. God's perfect relationship with His creation had been destroyed by sin.

So what does this story have to do with you and me today? Romans 5:12 says, "Therefore, just as sin entered the world through one man, and death through sin, and in this way death came to all men, because all sinned." This one scene introduced sin into the world, and it has been affecting humanity ever since. Humankind's relationship with God was broken, and we needed a new covenant with Him. Let's see how all of this started in Genesis 3.

Genesis 3:1-6; Romans 5:12-21

Everything was going so well in the Garden of Eden. But in Genesis 3:1, we see the first dilemma in all of human history: Satan asking Eve if God really said what she thought He said. Satan was attempting to get Adam and Eve to doubt God's Word. "Maybe God was not telling us the truth," they thought. And that's where sin began.

God's covenant with us starts with His Word. He makes promises to us, and we covenant to obey His commands. Whenever we doubt God's Word, we decide that we know what is best for our lives. When we disobey His commands—when we sin—the result is that we break covenant with God.

Read Romans 5:12-21. Paul describes how the broken covenant in Genesis 3 has affected all of humanity. Think about some sins that you struggle with. Then try to trace the root of those sins to doubting God's Word. What commands of God are you not trusting when you commit those sins?

Day 2 >>

Genesis 3:1-6; Genesis 11:1-9

Look again at Genesis 3:1-6. Why did Adam and Eve do what they did? Look closely at verse 5. Satan tempted Eve by saying, "You will be like God . . ." Eve wanted to be god over her own life. Adam and Eve wanted to make decisions without the help of God, even if that meant completely ignoring God's commands.

We do the same thing, don't we? We may not eat fruit from a forbidden tree, but when we sin, we play god. Our actions say that we know better than God. Read Genesis 11:1-9. Here, we see that God's creation wanted to make a name for themselves.

In tempting us to be god over our own lives, Satan tries to steal God's glory. When you disobey God, how is Satan tempting you to be god over your own life? As a result, how does your sin steal God's glory? Record your thoughts.

Day 3 >>>
Genesis 3:7; John 5:16-30

Read Genesis 3:7. The covenant had been broken. So what happened next? The first effect of Adam and Eve's sin was guilt; they immediately covered themselves. All people in the world, including you and me, have a sense of right and wrong. And we know when we mess up. That's the way Adam and Eve felt.

The rest of the Bible teaches that we all stand guilty before God. Read John 5:16-30. One day, we will stand before a perfect Judge—Jesus. The problem is: How can we stand before Jesus and be found innocent instead of guilty? And that's why we need to enter into a new covenant with God before we get there!

Think about the feelings of guilt you have felt at times in your relationship with God. How do you get rid of that guilt? Write a prayer to God asking Him to take away any guilt you may have in your life right now.

Day 4 >>>>>

Genesis 3:9-10; Romans 9:30-33

Read Genesis 3:9-10. When Adam and Eve knew God was coming, they immediately hid. Adam was too ashamed to be in the presence of God. And then in Genesis 3:10, he felt fear. When God spoke to him, Adam responded that he was afraid.

In some parts of the world, families and communities are so valued that bringing shame upon yourself is the worst thing you can do. In other parts of the world, fear is a consuming emotion. Some tribes in Africa perform rituals because they fear the gods they believe in.

Read Romans 9:30-33. Paul talks about those who trust in Jesus never being put to shame. Write down any ways you have experienced shame in your relationship with God because of sin. Do you ever find yourself fearing God as a result of your sin? Write a short prayer thanking Him

for sending Jesus so that we never have to know shame or fear again.

Day 5 >>>>>

Genesis 3:1-8; Matthew 4:1-11

Review Genesis 3:1-8. Now, look at Matthew 4:1-11. Jesus was tempted three times by the devil. Each time, he responded by quoting Scripture. Do you think Jesus had to quote Scripture in order to resist temptation? I don't think he did. I believe Jesus was setting a pattern for us. If doubting God's Word is the root of our sin, then knowing and trusting God's Word is the best strategy for fighting sin.

As you close out this week, go back to the list of sins that you are currently struggling with in your life. Find a Bible verse that deals with each one of those sins. Write these verses down, and begin memorizing them so that when you are tempted to sin in those ways, you can be like Jesus and quote God's Word. God's Word is the foundation for our covenant with Him. The more we know His Word, the more we will be able to grow in our relationship with Him.

Consequences

memory verse

"And I will put enmity between you and the woman, and between your offspring and hers; he will crush your head, and you will strike his heel."

Genesis 3:15

Remember the story of Derek Redmond? We left him lying injured on the track, unable to fulfill his dream of making it to the Olympic finals. But the story did not end there. Derek's dad came running down from the stands to help his son hobble the rest of the race. All the fans were on their feet cheering as Derek and his dad limped toward the finish line. It became one of the most memorable Olympic moments.

As we discussed last week, because of sin entering the world through Adam and Eve, we're all "down on the track," broken and injured. But the good news is that we have a Father who has come running to us. God has not left us alone in our sin.

This week we're going to look at how God responded to the sin of Adam and Eve. The picture is not pretty. Discipline is a major part of God's reaction to our sin. Adam and Eve would never be the same. They would experience pain and suffering in the world as a result of their sin. But when God pours out discipline, He also pours out grace. Let's see how God responded to Adam and Eve's sin, and let's think about how this relates to God's response to sin in our lives.

Genesis 3:9-10; Luke 15:11-20

Look back at Genesis 2:15-17. Remember that God told Adam if he ate from this tree, he would die. That was a steep consequence for one act of disobedience! But it reminds us of how serious sin is in God's sight. Now, read Genesis 3:9-10. God took the initiative to come to Adam even after he sinned.

Read Luke 15:11-20. Even after the prodigal son committed all kinds of sins, when he came home, his father ran toward him. In this parable, Jesus was giving a clear picture of a God who pursues us even when we don't deserve it.

Journal today about a time in your life when you disobeyed God but learned that He still cared for you and provided for you. How did that make you feel? What did you learn about God during that time? Thank God for faithfully pursuing you even when you are unfaithful to Him.

Day 2 ››

Genesis 3:11-12, 17-19; Romans 6:19-23

The first person God confronted in Genesis 3 was Adam. What did Adam do? He blamed someone else for his sin. First, he blamed Eve. But Adam also blamed God. He told God that He was the One who put Eve there with him.

We don't like to admit we are wrong, and we all have a tendency to shift the responsibility for our sin to someone else. Read Romans 6:19-23. The punishment for our sins belongs to us, and that punishment is death. That's exactly what God showed Adam in Genesis 3:17-19. When you break covenant with a perfect and holy God and sin against Him, the result is divine discipline.

Spend some time today in confession of your sin before God. Resist the tendency to blame someone else for your sin. Write a simple prayer asking God to forgive you. Then write a prayer thanking Him for His gift of eternal life.

Day 3 >>>

Genesis 3:13, 16; 2 Corinthians 11:3-4

The second person God confronted in Genesis 3 was Eve. Like Adam, she tried to play the blame game. But that didn't mean she was off the hook. Read Genesis 3:16 to see God's punishment of Eve. Her sin would dramatically affect her relationships with her children and husband.

Read 2 Corinthians 11:3-4. Paul warned these Christians that their fate might be just like Eve's. We may think sin will bring us more pleasure, but in the end, sin only takes away the pleasure God has designed for our lives. Journal today about a time when you thought doing a particular sin would bring you pleasure but later you realized you had been deceived. What did this circumstance teach you about God's discipline? Pray that God will help you trust Him when Satan attempts to deceive you and pull you away from God.

Day 4 »»»
Genesis 3:14-15; Revelation 20:1-10

I hate snakes. I spent two weeks in Sudan recently. Some of the deadliest snakes in the world live there. The whole time, I was constantly on the lookout for snakes. I knew one bite could mean an early exit from this earth for me!

Read Genesis 3:14-15. After God confronted Adam and Eve, he confronted the snake. Before we go on, read Revelation 20:1-10. Here the serpent is equated with Satan. What God said to the snake in Genesis applied to Satan and all of his demons. There will be a constant struggle between humankind and Satan. But don't miss the promise in verse 15! This is a picture of what would be fulfilled when Jesus died on the cross and rose from the grave. He has conquered Satan, sin, and death; and as a result, we can have eternal life!

Journal today about all that God has saved you from. Thank Him for His salvation, and praise Jesus for the victory

He won over Satan, sin, and death. Then, spend some time memorizing Genesis 3:15.

Day 5 >>>>>

Genesis 3:21; Luke 15:21-24

This week's passage ends with God clothing Adam and Eve. We have learned how God disciplined sin. Adam and Eve deserved to be cast out of God's presence forever, never to experience His love again. But that is not what God did. Instead, He made them clothes as a covering for their guilt, shame, and fear.

Read Luke 15:21-24. (You read the first part of this story earlier in the week.) Notice how the father welcomed the prodigal son. The first thing he did was to put a robe on him. The son didn't deserve this kind of treatment. The father showed him grace anyway. Remember that grace is always the foundation of our covenant relationship with God.

Write out some ways in which God has shown His grace in your life. Write Him a prayer thanking Him for clothing you with the righteousness of Christ even though you don't deserve it.

covenant: Knowing God—His Relationship With His People

The Flood

memory verse

"I am going to bring floodwaters on the earth to destroy all life under the heavens, every creature that has the breath of life in it. Everything on earth will perish. But I will establish my covenant with you, and you will enter the ark—you and your sons and your wife and your sons' wives with you." **Genesis 6:17-18**

I applied for a variety of scholarships my senior year of high school. I remember one of the scholarships was for the cost of tuition, books, housing, and food. I sent in the application, and then they asked me to come for an interview. After the interview, I was told I would receive a letter in the mail letting me know if I had gotten it or not.

I waited for what felt like forever. I was so excited when the letter finally arrived. I braced myself for the news. I opened the envelope and saw the first word on the letter—"Congratulations." I was so pumped that I couldn't contain myself. I took off running around the house, jumping up and down, shouting in celebration. I was so glad to be chosen.

This week, we're going to look at the first actual mention of the word "covenant" in the Bible. And the person God chose to initiate covenant with was Noah. As we study this week's passage, we're going to see the reason God sent the flood. But I don't believe that's the primary purpose of why this story is in the Bible. I believe that God is primarily showing us why He chose Noah for the first covenant in the Bible. So as we study together this week, we'll have the opportunity to read different Scriptures, journal, and pray so that we might be found faithful before God, just as Noah was.

Day 1 >

Genesis 6:11-13; Romans 1:28-32

Extreme sports have grown in popularity over the last few years. Snowboarding, BMX, and skateboarding are just a few of the events that have taken sports to a new level. In Genesis 6:11-13, we're going to see extreme discipline. Last week, we looked at God's discipline of Adam, Eve, and the serpent. Now, we're going to see discipline at a new level. God is going to flood the entire earth.

God did this because the people had become violent and corrupt. Read Romans 1:28-32. The descriptions sound similar, don't they? The people during Noah's day had earned God's discipline. As we have already discussed, because God is holy and just, His discipline is extremely serious.

Journal today about times when you have seen God's discipline in your own life. Do you believe God's extreme discipline is a sign of God's extreme love for us? Pray that God will help you to understand the value of His discipline in your life.

Day 2 >>

Genesis 6:9-10; Psalm 7:6-17

Why did God choose Noah for a covenant relationship? Amid the violence and corruption of the people in the world, Noah stood out. Read Genesis 6:9. How is Noah described? Righteous. This means that he was blameless before God, avoiding sin and pursuing a life of holiness.

Read Psalm 7:6-17 to see another picture of the contrast between those who are righteous and those who are sinful. This Psalm shows us that God is righteous, and He wants His character to be reflected in His people. Noah stood out in his day because of his holiness in an unholy world.

What are some ways you can stand out with holiness in an unholy world? We don't do this so that we can be better than everyone else but because we want to show the character of God to those around us. Write some ways you can show the righteousness of God today. Then pray God will use you to put His character on display.

Day 3 >>>
Genesis 6:9-10; Micah 6:6-8

Genesis 6:9-10 teaches that Noah "walked with God." Flip over to Micah 6:6-8, and read why this was important. Micah asked the question, "How do we know and worship God?" The answer is simple: We know and worship God when we walk with Him.

You show people they are important by hanging out with them, walking with them, listening to them, sharing your life with them. And that's what a covenant with God is all about. Noah found grace in

God's eyes as he walked with God. By walking with God, we, too, can experience His grace and favor.

Write three things you can do today to walk more closely with God. Try taking a walk around your neighborhood while praying the whole way, as if you were talking with a friend. It may seem a little weird at first, but it will help you begin to experience "walking with God" in a fresh way!

Day 4 >>>>

Genesis 6:14-21; Proverbs 3:5-6

Read Genesis 6:14-21. God gave Noah very specific instructions for building the ark. Pay close attention to verse 18, because this is the first time we actually see "covenant" mentioned in the Bible. God once again provided for all of the terms of the covenant. All that is left is for Noah to trust in the faithfulness of the God who is making the covenant.

Read Proverbs 3:5-6. Trust is a central part of our covenant relationship with God. Our understanding of our lives is very limited. Noah probably couldn't imagine what was about to happen. But Noah did have God's promise that he and his family would be saved from destruction. How has God shown His faithfulness to you recently?

Write a specific circumstance in which you trusted God and leaned "not on your own

covenant: Knowing God—His Relationship With His People

understanding." Pray that God will help you to trust Him more as you grow deeper in your relationship with Him.

Day 5 »»»»

Genesis 6:22; Exodus 14:12-33

Read Genesis 6:22. Noah did exactly what God had told him to do. We have already seen the extreme discipline in this passage. Now we see extreme obedience. Why did God choose to pour out His grace on Noah in this covenant? Because Noah was ready to obey God.

Read about Moses in Exodus 14:12-33. Underline every time Moses did something just as God commanded him. You should find several twhere this is mentioned. A covenant with God requires extreme obedience to His commands.

We've seen four characteristics of Noah this week. He was righteous, he walked with God, he trusted God, and he was obedient. Which of these characteristics do you most need to work on? Write some ways you can be more faithful in your covenant with God. Pray that God would help you better develop these characteristics in your life.

God's Covenant With Noah

memory verse

"I establish my covenant with you: Never again will all life be cut off by the waters of a flood; never again will there be a flood to destroy the earth." **Genesis 9:11**

On August 29, 2005, Hurricane Katrina hit the Gulf Coast. Homes were destroyed, and thousands of lives were ruined. Floodwaters filled New Orleans, where I lived. Luckily, we had evacuated. But my wife and I lost almost everything. The church where I served on staff, Edgewater Baptist Church, was Underwater Baptist Church!

About a month later, we returned to our house and church. Both had been filled with about nine feet of water. Everything was destroyed. Some items had floated outside while others were completely missing. Every building in our neighborhood had spray paint on the side to indicate whether or not rescue crews had found people in each side. I will never forget that site.

Having seen this, I still cannot imagine what it must have been like when God flooded the earth. Except for Noah, his family, and a bunch of animals he had with him, everything else on the earth was dead. And in the middle of this "dead" scene God initiates his first official covenant with man. Sometimes, God's grace is brightest in the darkest times. Let's look this week at what was involved in Noah's covenant with God and think about how it applies to our lives today.

Genesis 9:1-7; Psalm 51:10-12

Have you ever messed up and wished you could just start over? While we can't go back in time, the Bible teaches us that God desires to restore us after we fall. Read about God's blessing on Noah and his family in Genesis 9:1-7. Compare this with Genesis 1:26-28. They're similar, right? After the flood, God was restoring His people to what He had originally created them to be.

We are restored through our covenant with God. No, we can't go back in time and do things over again, but we can be forgiven. Read Psalm 51:10-12. After David had sinned against God, he asked God to restore the joy of His salvation to him.

Do any areas of your life need to be restored by God? Write a prayer similar to Psalm 51 asking for forgiveness of your sins and for God to restore His blessing in your life.

Genesis 8:20-22; Hebrews 10:3-10

Read Genesis 8:20-22. As Noah entered into covenant with God, he built an altar to sacrifice burnt offerings. We're going to see this over and over in the Old Testament as God entered into covenant with people. That's because covenant involves sacrifice.

Sacrifices in the Old Testament were pleasing to God and led to His forgiveness for sins.

What's really cool, though, is when you realize the significance of sacrifice in the New Testament. Read Hebrews 10:3-10. These verses show us that Jesus' sacrifice on the cross was exactly what we needed in order to be in a relationship with God. His sacrifice made our covenant with God possible.

Jesus made this sacrifice for all people. Think about someone today who you can tell about Jesus. Then write a prayer to God asking Him to give you an opportunity to share how Jesus paid the price for our sins with His sacrifice on a cross.

Day 3 >>>

Genesis 9:8-11; John 10:7-10

Let's read Genesis 9:8-11. Look at the end of verse 11. God promised that He would never destroy the earth with a flood again. In other words, what happened in New Orleans won't ever happen to the whole earth again. This is good news!

God made this promise out of love for His creation. He longs for us to have the most abundant life possible. Check out John 10:7-10. In those verses, Jesus said that He came to give life to the full. When we place our faith in Him, we can know He wants

covenant: Knowing God—His Relationship With His People

us to be completely fulfilled. And we can also know that nothing in this world can ever take away that satisfaction from us. Now, that's an incredible promise!

Write down three ways Jesus has given you fulfillment in your life. Pray today that, even when life brings you difficult circumstances, God will help you to be satisfied in Him. Ask God to help you move toward a more focused walk with Him today.

Day 4

Genesis 9:12-15; Ezekiel 1:25-28

Why is an engagement ring or wedding ring so important? Because of what it signifies. It's a symbol of a covenant. One look at a person's hand reminds her of a commitment to her spouse.

Many times, when God makes covenants with His people in the Bible, He gives them a sign. Read Genesis 9:12-15. Then read in Ezekiel 1:25-28 about how the rainbow stands for the glory of God. This sign is still evident today. After Hurricane Katrina had passed, rainbows could be seen all along the Gulf Coast. This was a sign that God is still faithful to His covenant.

God gives us many reminders of His commitment to us. List some of those reminders. Then try to list some things you can do to express your commitment to Him. Ask God to help you live your life as a sign of that commitment.

Day 5 >>>>>

Genesis 9:16-17; John 4:1-14

Read Genesis 9:16-17. Circle the word "everlasting." God told Noah that His covenant would never be broken. This is very similar to what Jesus said to the woman at the well in John 4:1-14. Jesus told her that when she drank from His living water, she would never be thirsty again. God's covenant with this woman would be everlasting.

This is good news. Think about how it affects our lives. When my home was flooded and all of my possessions were destroyed, I didn't have to worry. Why not? Because our covenant with God lasts forever! In the big picture, I know God will take care of me.

How does God's everlasting covenant with you affect your perspective on things that happen in your life? You might write about a difficult time that you have experienced recently. Then reflect on God's everlasting covenant and thank Him for His promise of eternal life.

God's Covenant with Abraham

memory verse

He took him outside and said, "Look up at the heavens and count the stars—if indeed you can count them." Then he said to him, "So shall your offspring be." Abram believed the LORD, and he credited it to him as righteousness. **Genesis 15:5-6**

A blind leap. An uncertain next step. Going where no man has gone before! These are some of the images that come to mind when people think about faith. "Faith," some people say, "is taking a blind leap into the unknown." As inspiring as that may sound, I just don't believe it's true. Faith in God is not a blind leap.

When we place our faith in God, we are not stepping out into the unknown. Instead, we are stepping out on the dependable, proven, always-trustworthy promises of the God of the universe. When God calls us to trust Him and tells us to do something, we don't act based on some faint hope that He is going to come through on His Word. Instead, we know He's going to come through; He's going to provide for us as we put our faith in Him.

This week we're going to look in Genesis 15 at God's covenant with Abram (whom God later renamed Abraham). We're going to see an incredible picture of faith. Our memory verse for the week says Abram's faith was credited to him as righteousness. The effects of this kind of faith are huge for our lives today. In fact, Paul tells us in Romans 4:23-24 that the words spoken to Abraham in Genesis 15 were not just written for him but also for us. God will credit righteousness to us the same way. Let's take a journey this week through Genesis 15 and discover what faith is really all about.

Day 1 >

Genesis 15:1; 1 Kings 17:1-16

"How do I know God's will for my life?" This is one of the most common questions among Christians. We have this idea that God is hiding His will for our lives and we have to try to find it. This is simply not true. God has revealed His will for our lives in His Word.

Read Genesis 15:1. Note that "the word of the Lord" came to Abram. Now read 1 Kings 17:1-16. Underline every time you see "the word of the Lord" mentioned. When God establishes His covenant and directs the lives of His people, He always does it through His Word. Do you really want to know God's will for your life? Then read His Word, and let it be the foundation for how you relate to God.

Begin today by memorizing Genesis 15:5-6. Write some ways that knowing God's Word will help you know His will. Pray that God will help you to understand His Word so you can follow His will.

Day 2 >>

Genesis 15:1-3; Matthew 28:5-10

The first words God said to Abram were, "Do not be afraid." Why was Abram afraid? God had promised him many sons and daughters (Gen. 12:1-3). But Abram was starting to get old, and he still didn't have

covenant: Knowing God—His Relationship With His People

a son! He was beginning to wonder if God would keep His promise.

God's covenant with Abram teaches us that sometimes faith involves waiting for God's timing. Read Matthew 28:5-10. Imagine the confusion when the followers of Jesus saw Him die on the cross and be buried in a tomb. They must have thought, "What is God doing?" But the angel says the same thing to them that God said to Abram: "Do not be afraid."

Journal about a time when God worked in your life in a way you would not have planned. How did that affect your relationship with Him? What did you learn about faith during that time? Ask God to help you trust Him even when things are not going as you planned.

Day 3

Genesis 15:4-6; Isaiah 40:25-31

So how did God take Abram's fear away? He took him outside and told him to try to count the stars in the sky. That was the number of sons and daughters he was going to have. Wow! What a promise for an old guy who didn't even have a child yet!

Read Isaiah 40:25-31. See how God brings out the stars one by one and calls them each by name. What an awesome thought! If He is able to bring the stars out, and if He has named each one of them, then He certainly has the power to fulfill His promise to Abram. He certainly has the power to keep His promises to us.

Write about a time when God showed you His faithfulness and power. How does His faithfulness in the past help you trust Him for the future? Pray that God will give you deeper knowledge of His greatness so that your faith in Him can increase.

Day 4 >>>>
Genesis 15:7-16;
Hebrews 11:13-16

Read Genesis 15:7-16. God's promise to Abram was not just for his lifetime but also for many people who would come after him. God promised Abram that his people would live in the land where he was at that time, but Abram would not live to see that day.

Now read Hebrews 11:13-16. These verses describe a similar picture. We can trust God will be faithful to His covenant, even though we may not see all the rewards of our faith while we are on this earth. The Bible teaches that one day Jesus is going to come back to this earth. It could happen today or tomorrow! But it's also possible that we will die before that happens.

Imagine: What if you were in Abram's position? How could you learn to trust God even when you weren't sure that you would live to see all of His promises fulfilled? Then journal about how this might apply to your life as well.

Day 5 >>>>>

Genesis 15:17-21; Isaiah 43:1-7

God sealed His covenant with Abram through a ritual in Genesis 15:17-21. This was an ancient form of making an agreement between two people. The ritual symbolized God's presence with His people and protection of them.

The good news is that we don't have to follow the same ritual to enter into a covenant with God. You don't need to go out and cut a goat and ram into two pieces! But the symbolism is still the same for our lives today. When we enter into a relationship with God, we receive the promise of His presence and His protection. Read Isaiah 43:1-7 to see these same promises of God for His people.

Look through your Bible, and write some verses where God promises either His presence or His protection. What difference do these promises make in your life? Pray that God will make you more aware of His presence and His protection in your life today.

The Covenant Sign

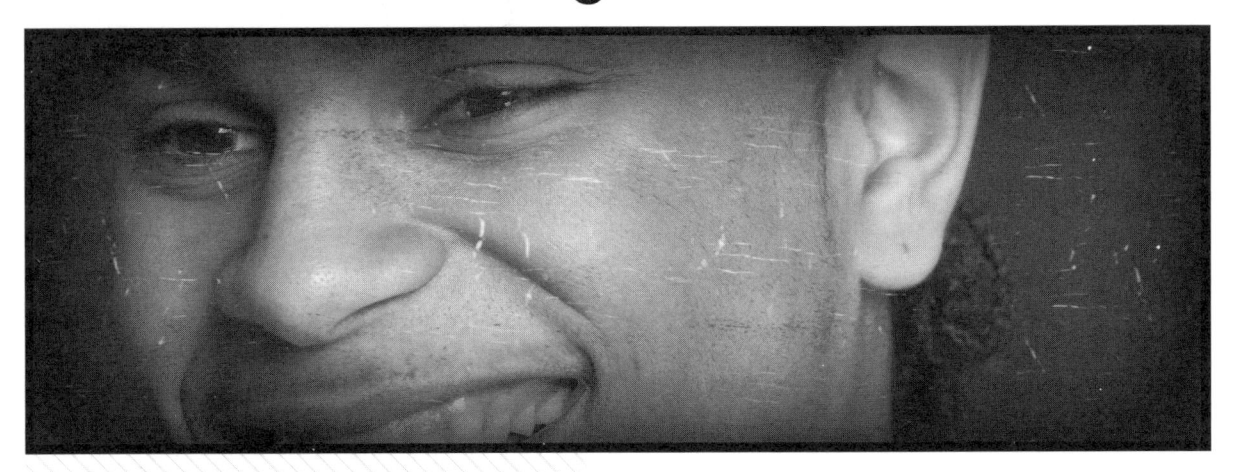

memory verse

"I will establish my covenant as an everlasting covenant between me and you and your descendants after you for the generations to come, to be your God and the God of your descendants after you." **Genesis 17:7**

There are places in the world where it is illegal to be a Christian. I remember when I was once in one of those places. I was teaching about baptism. Two guys wanted to be baptized. "When we are baptized," I told them, "we publicly identify with Christ and with His Church. I realize that being baptized in your country may cost you your life." The first guy said, "I have sacrificed everything to follow Jesus. I want to be baptized." The second guy, a teenager, said boldly, "Jesus is my Lord. Whatever He says to do, I will do." I baptized these two men in a bathtub in the back of the house.

Is baptism important enough to risk your life in order to do it? Scripture says it is. Jesus commands us to be baptized as a symbol of our relationship with God through Him. The foundation for this symbol is found in the Old Testament.

This week we'll look at the sign of God's covenant with His people in Genesis 17:1-27. We're going to see the importance of an outward symbol that represents our relationship with God. We'll learn more about covenant and discover the importance of baptism in our Christian lives. But before we begin, I invite you to pray in your heart the same thing prayed by the teenager I mentioned earlier: "Lord, whatever you want me to do, I will do." After you pray that prayer, you're ready to dive into Genesis 17.

covenant: Knowing God—His Relationship With His People

Genesis 17:1-9; Matthew 1:1-17

There are two parts to every covenant: God's part and humanity's part. Read Genesis 17:1-9. Look for God's role and Abraham's role. God's role is similar to what we saw in Genesis 15. He promises Abraham many sons and daughters (vv. 4-6). He promises Abraham that He will be faithful to His promise (vv. 7-8). But in verse 6, God promises something we haven't seen yet—that Abraham's many descendants will include kings.

Read Matthew 1:1-17. Why does the Bible have long lists of names like this? Notice that Matthew 1 starts with Abraham, then leads to King David, and ultimately leads to King Jesus. The Bible is showing us that God really is faithful to keep His promises!

Start today by making a list of three promises from God's Word that you can trust in this week. As the week goes on, write how you see God keeping those promises. Thank God for His eternal faithfulness to Abraham and His eternal faithfulness to you.

Genesis 17:1-9; Daniel 7:26-27

Yesterday, we looked at God's part in the covenant. Now let's look at Abraham's part. Read Genesis 17:1-9. In verse 1, God tells

Abraham to walk with Him and to be blameless. In verse 9, God tells Abraham he must keep this covenant. Abraham's part in the covenant is to be obedient to God's commands.

Read Daniel 7:26-27. See what all the rulers mentioned in this passage will one day do? They will worship and obey God. This is our natural response to a covenant with God. We are so overwhelmed by His presence that we fall on our faces and worship Him. Then we rise up, committed to obeying Him.

In your prayer time today, try praying on your knees, possibly even with your face to the ground. This is a posture that shows our reverence and respect for God. After you finish, rise and write at least one way you will specifically obey God today.

Day 3 >>>

Genesis 17:5, 15-16; John 1:40-42

Names in the Bible were important because of what they symbolized. Read Genesis 17:5, 15-16. Abram and Sarai's names were changed to signify that they would be the father and mother of many nations. Read John 1:40-42. Jesus changed Peter's name from Simon to Peter, meaning "rock." Later, Jesus would show the significance of Peter's name change (see Matt. 16:17-20).

Our names may not change when we enter into covenant with God, but in many ways, our identities totally change. Our lives are completely different because of our relationship with God.

Write a list of three to five changes that took place when you entered into a relationship with God. Then write some changes that are still taking place in your Christian life right now. Ask God to continue to transform your identity to be more like Him.

Day 4

Genesis 17:10-14; Romans 4:9-12

Here's an interesting part of Genesis 17. God established circumcision as a sign of His covenant with Abraham. Circumcision was a physical symbol that the Israelites had entered into a covenant with God. It would be a reminder that God had made promises to them and that they had committed to worship and obey Him.

Now read Romans 4:9-12. Paul taught that circumcision didn't make Abraham righteous. Instead, circumcision was a sign of Abraham's righteousness by faith. Similarly, baptism is the New Testament sign of our covenant with God. Just like circumcision didn't bring righteousness, we don't have to be baptized in order to be saved. Instead, it's a crucial sign of the faith we have placed in Jesus.

Have you been baptized? If not, what is keeping you from obeying this important command from Jesus? Write down what you believe baptism symbolizes about your relationship with God. Next time you see someone baptized, remember the importance of this physical sign of our faith.

Day 5 >>>>>

Genesis 17:17-27; Acts 2:36-41

Welcome to the family! The sign of circumcision in the Old Testament was a unique symbol that identified the men of Israel as members of God's family. Read in Genesis 17:17-27 how this promise was reserved for the family of Abraham, which would eventually become the people of Israel.

Read Acts 2:36-41. In the first Christian sermon, Peter told the people to repent and be baptized. Thousands of people were baptized. The New Testament church was started. Not only is baptism a symbol of our covenant with God, but it also shows we're a part of God's family.

Based on our study of Genesis 17, list the reasons circumcision was so important for Abraham's family. Then list the reasons baptism is so important for us today. Pray that God will help you understand the significance of this sign of your covenant with Him and your membership in His family.

The Passover

At midnight the LORD struck down all the firstborn in Egypt, from the firstborn of Pharaoh, who sat on the throne, to the firstborn of the prisoner, who was in the dungeon, and the firstborn of all the livestock as well. **Exodus 12:29**

Eighth grade was the first year at my school that you could try out for the basketball team. I thought everyone on the basketball team was cool. I wanted to be cool, so I decided to try out. The only problem was that I was the shortest kid in my class. How could I impress the coach enough for him to put me on the team?

A couple of weeks before tryouts while reading my Bible, I came across Luke 1:37, which says, "For nothing is impossible with God." It seemed like the words of Scripture leaped off the page and into my heart. I knew I could make the team.

You see, I had this idea that if I could only muster up enough faith, then I could do anything. The only problem was that my faith was in my ability to impress everyone at tryouts (and, by the way, I wasn't very impressive). It really doesn't matter if you have great faith if it's aimed at the wrong things; what we need is faith in a great God.

Our God is able to do the impossible. We're going to see that in the Book of Exodus this week. What we will notice is that just a little bit of faith in our great God goes a long way. Let's take a look at the story of the exodus of God's people from Egypt and the feast of the Passover. As we do, let's think about how this story teaches us to put our faith in God.

Day 1 >

Exodus 12:31-32;
Matthew 17:20-21

The Israelites were slaves in Egypt, but God had a plan to make Pharaoh let them go. God sent all sorts of natural disasters and plagues. Yet Pharaoh still would not free the Israelites. In the end, God sent a plague on all the firstborn children of Egypt, and what seemed impossible finally happened. Pharaoh commanded the Israelites to leave Egypt.

We may face circumstances that look hopeless. But Jesus says in Matthew 17:20-21 that a little bit of faith in God can move mountains. We can trust in God because, ultimately, He delivers His people.

Think about a time in the past when God has provided for you to bring you out of a difficult situation. What did you learn about God during that time? Pray that God will give you the strength to face every circumstance in life with complete trust in Him.

Day 2 >>

Exodus 12:33-39; Matthew 6:25-33

God takes care of all of the details. As the Israelites left Egypt, they left with plenty of food, clothing, silver, and gold. The Egyptians actually gave away all of these things to the people who had been their slaves!

covenant: Knowing God—His Relationship With His People

Read Matthew 6:25-33. In these verses, Jesus promised that our Heavenly Father would care for every detail of our lives. He will provide for our every need; what we must do is seek Him with all of our hearts.

Record what it means to you to seek God with all of your heart? How does that help you to trust Him to provide for you? Spend some time praying for some specific needs in your life. Then, after you pray, trust God to not only hear your prayers but also to answer them according to everything you need.

Day 3 >>>

Exodus 12:38; Exodus 14:1-21

When God shows His faithfulness to us, He is also showing His faithfulness to others. Take a look at Exodus 12:38. The Bible says that "many other people" left with the Israelites. They had seen God's faithfulness to His people and decided to trust in God.

Read Exodus 14:1-21. This is the story of God taking His people through the Red Sea. Why did God perform this miracle? He did the impossible for His people so that the Egyptians would know He is the Lord and He is faithful (see 14:4 and 14:18).

People will place belief in God after seeing His faithfulness to us. How does this relate to you? God provides so that people around us will see His love and goodness.

Write a story of a time God showed His faithfulness to you. Then find someone who doesn't know the Lord, and share with that person. Pray that God will use you to show His faithfulness.

Day 4 >>>>

Exodus 12:40-42; Deuteronomy 6:1-8

Read Exodus 12:40-42. Notice that these verses are similar to the promise God gave Abraham in Genesis 15:13-14. Just as He had promised, God delivered His people. Read Deuteronomy 16:1-8. The Israelites remembered what happened in Exodus 12. What God did for His people in Exodus 12 had been promised many years before and would be remembered for a long time to come.

Even thousands of years later, we're still talking about the Passover and the covenant God continued with His people on that day. God's covenant relationship with His people never stops. This is just as true for us as it was for the Israelites.

Spend some time thinking about your future. What do you envision happening in your life over the next year, or two years, or five years? Write out a prayer to God thanking Him for the faithfulness He is going to show you and committing your obedience to Him in the future.

Exodus 12:43-51;
1 Corinthians 5:6-8

What exactly was the Passover? The angel of the Lord went to every house in Egypt and struck down the firstborn son. But the Israelites had sprinkled a lamb's blood above each of their doorposts. The angel saw the blood and "passed over" the houses. The firstborn sons were spared.

Read 1 Corinthians 5:6-8. These verses tell us that Christ is our Passover Lamb. By the blood He shed on the cross, we do not have to experience the judgment of God. It is so important for us to reflect often on how Jesus has saved us from our sins.

How can you celebrate the forgiveness of your sins through Jesus? Maybe you can read through the story of His crucifixion in the Gospels. Maybe you can write to Him some words of praise, thanking Him for making a way for us to be united with a holy and loving God! Whatever you decide, take a moment to honestly express your thankfulness to your Savior.

God's Covenant with Moses

memory verse

Then he took the Book of the Covenant and read it to the people. They responded, "We will do everything the LORD has said; we will obey."
Exodus 24:7

I made the eighth-grade basketball team. It didn't make me cool, but it made one girl think I was. Her name was Melanie. I really wanted to show her that I was an incredible basketball player.

The next game, I had my chance to show Melanie how great I was. Early in the game I had two free throws. I made the first shot. "Melanie is loving me now," I thought. I took the ball for my second free throw. I shot it. Air ball. The coach immediately put me on the bench! I got to school the next day, and Melanie ignored me. Ouch!

Read the Bible, and you'll learn you can't earn the love of God. God gives His love freely. That's what grace is all about. At the same time, our obedience to Him is an essential part of our relationship. After the Israelites came out of Egypt, they began to disobey God. They were breaking their side of their covenant with God.

When we come to Exodus 24:1-8, we see God renewing His covenant with His people through Moses. The important features of God's covenant with Moses are the blood of the sacrifice and the obedience of the people. Let's study Exodus 24 to understand the importance of His blood and our obedience.

covenant: Knowing God—His Relationship With His People

Exodus 24:1-8; Genesis 8:20-9:11

One of the characteristics of God's Word is its unity. The various stories in the Bible all work together to tell one main story. Let's look at an example.

Read Exodus 24:1-8. Then read Genesis 8:20-9:11, the passage about Noah that we studied a few weeks ago. Make a list in your journal of the similarities between these two covenants. Both covenants were cause for celebration. Noah had been saved from the flood, and the Israelites had been brought out of slavery. Both covenants involved a sacrifice. In both covenants God gave promises of His presence and protection. And in both covenants, God called the people to obey His commands.

These characteristics are present in our covenant with God today. Take a moment to write how each characteristic is present in the way you relate to God. Then pray that God will help you to be faithful to His covenant with you.

Exodus 24:1-2; Hebrews 12:22-24

Have you ever heard of a matchmaker? You know, someone who likes to bring couples together? Well, in this passage, Moses is kind of like a matchmaker. The term the Old Testament uses is mediator. Read

Exodus 24:1-2. Notice that Moses was the only one who could approach the Lord. He had the responsibility of connecting the Israelites with God and His Word.

Read Hebrews 12:22-24. Moses as the mediator for the Israelites foreshadowed Jesus as mediator of the New Covenant. You see, God is too holy and too awesome—and we are too sinful—for us to approach Him on our own. Jesus plays the role of mediator, allowing us to have access to God. This is the foundation for why and how we can pray.

Write what you think it means to pray in Jesus' name. How does this affect how you pray? As you spend some time in prayer today, thank Jesus for being your mediator.

Day 3 >>>

Exodus 24:3-6; Hebrews 9:16-22

We said at the beginning of the week that blood was going to be really important in this covenant between God and Moses. After reading Exodus 24:3-6, we see one of the two primary purposes of the blood sacrifice. First, it was sprinkled on the altar. This was a sign of God's forgiveness for the people's sins. Why was the blood necessary?

Read Hebrews 9:16-22. Here we see that the shedding of blood was necessary for our forgiveness. That's why Jesus had to die on the cross. He couldn't have just come to the earth, lived a perfect life, and then gone back to heaven without shedding His blood for our sins. If He hadn't gone to the cross, we couldn't be forgiven.

Write a prayer of confession to God today. Confess your need for Him, and confess the sins that you have been holding on to.

Day 4

Exodus 24:7; Hebrews 2:14-18

How does the blood of the sacrifice relate to our obedience? We've already said that we don't obey God in order to earn His grace. We obey God because of His grace. Let's look at this a little deeper.

When the blood was sprinkled on the altar and the people, they said, "We will do everything the Lord has said; we will obey." But we know from the reading we've done over the last few weeks that the people didn't obey. The blood of the sacrifice served as a temporary pardon for sins. It did not give them the power to obey. Read Hebrews 2:14-18. With the blood Jesus shed on the cross He once and for all cleansed our sins. More than that, He destroyed the power of sin in our lives. We are able to live godly lives because of the blood shed by Christ.

Yesterday, you wrote out a prayer of confession. Today, write a prayer of obedience. Commit to following specific commands of God in your life, and ask for His grace to enable you to obey.

Day 5 >>>>>

Exodus 24:8; Matthew 26:26-30

In the Old Testament, we see a picture that will be completed by Jesus' life in the New Testament. Exodus 24:8 is one of those pictures. Here Moses talked about the blood of the covenant. Read Matthew 26:26-30. This is the story of the meal Jesus had with his disciples right before He went to the cross. In verse 28, Jesus said something similar to what Moses had said in Exodus 24.

The blood of the covenant in Exodus 24 was important for God's forgiveness of His people's sin. In Matthew 26, the same is true. With belief in Jesus' death on the cross, the disciples would be forgiven of their sins and they'd have the power to live godly lives.

How has Jesus completed your life? How has a relationship with Him enabled you to be more godly? Record your thoughts. Close this week by memorizing Exodus 24:8 and then praying that God, by His grace, will make you obedient to His covenant with you.

covenant: Knowing God—His Relationship With His People

God's Covenant with David

memory verse

"Your house and your kingdom will endure forever before me; your throne will be established forever." **2 Samuel 7:16**

"**I** have decided to make Jesus Lord of my life." This is a phrase used to describe the decision to believe in Christ. I have heard students who, after they prayed and received Christ into their hearts, said, "I have made Jesus Lord of my life." Others who make decisions to "rededicate" their lives to God say, "I have renewed my commitment to make Jesus Lord of my life."

The statements sound good, but they may not be totally accurate. Matthew 28:18 tells us that Jesus has all authority in heaven and earth. Philippians 2:9-11 tells us that one day every knee will bow (in heaven, earth, and under the earth) and every tongue will confess that Jesus is Lord. Jesus is Lord over everything, including our lives. When someone says, "I have decided to make Jesus Lord of my life," I think, "Jesus has always been Lord of your life and always will be. The question is: Have you submitted your life to His lordship?" One day, everyone will bow at Jesus' feet and call Him Lord. Will we surrender to His lordship now, or will we bow at His feet when it is too late?

Jesus will one day rule as Lord and King over everything. As we study 2 Samuel 7, we'll examine God's covenant with David. We are also going to see how God promised David to send a King through his line who would reign forever in His Kingdom. That King is Jesus.

Day 1 >

2 Samuel 7:8-17; Genesis 17:1-8

Let's start this week by comparing this covenant with a covenant we have already studied. Read Genesis 17:1-8. Then read 2 Samuel 7:8-17. Take a moment to write at least three similarities between these two covenants.

In the covenants with Abraham and David, God promised to bless their names (2 Sam. 7:9; Gen. 17:5). God promised that they would have land (2 Sam. 7:10; Gen. 17:8). God promised that kings would come from both their lines (2 Sam. 7:12-13; Gen. 17:6). Finally, God promised both Abraham and David that His covenant with them would be everlasting (2 Sam. 7:16; Gen. 17:7). God was establishing a pattern in His covenants, and that pattern affects our covenant with Him today.

Journal today about ways these similarities are evident in your relationship with God today. How has God established His covenant in the same way with you? Begin working on memorizing the memory verse for this week, 2 Samuel 7:16.

Day 2 >>

2 Samuel 7:8-11; Ephesians 2:1-10

In 2 Samuel 7:8-11, God spoke with David about the changes He had made in Davids life. He reminded David of all that He had given Him. Then God gave David promises to trust for the rest of his life.

Read Ephesians 2:1-10. These verses talk about the changes God makes in our lives through Jesus. We were dead, but now we're alive. We were deserving of God's wrath, but now He has shown us His mercy. We were destined for hell, but now we will be with Christ in heaven. When we trust Jesus for salvation, we are never the same again!

Write the following sentence three times: "I was _____, but now I am _____." Fill in the blanks with what you were before Christ and what you are now because of Christ. Then thank Him for the change He has brought in your life, just like in His covenant with David.

Day 3 >>>

2 Samuel 7:9; Genesis 11:1-9

Our culture pressures us to make a name for ourselves. We need to be the best athlete, the most talented musician, the smartest student, and so on. So much importance is placed on being the star of the show.

Read Genesis 11:1-9. Remember this story? The people were trying to make a name for themselves. Read God's promise to David in 2 Samuel 7:9. When we are in covenant with God, we don't have to worry about making a name for ourselves. God told David, "I will make your name great." God was telling David to trust Him. When we follow God, He will bless our lives in ways we never could imagine.

How can your desire to make a name for yourself sometimes keep you from experiencing God's full blessing? Write what you can do in your life to trust God to take care of you. Then pray that God's name will be exalted because of His blessings on your name.

Day 4 >>>>
2 Samuel 7:11-16; Galatians 3:15-25

Read 2 Samuel 7:11-16. God was promising David that he would have a son who would succeed him as king. The next king would be Solomon. But remember, this Kingdom is everlasting, right? Solomon died, so how could God have established the throne of His Kingdom forever?

That's where Jesus comes in. Read Galatians 3:15-25. When God spoke about "seed" and "offspring" in these Old Testament covenants, He was referring ultimately to Jesus, who would come from both the family of Abraham and David. The Old Testament contains so many promises that point us to Jesus! As you journal today, think about how valuable the Old Testament is for helping us know, understand, and love Jesus. Why is it important to know as much as we can about Jesus? Praise God for His faithfulness in sending Jesus as the King who would save us from our sins, just as He promised in the Old Testament.

Day 5

2 Samuel 7:16; Revelation 5:1-14

David was a godly man, a man after God's own heart. God used David to lead the nation of Israel through great times of prosperity. But just like every other person in history, he sinned. He failed as a leader at times. And ultimately, he died.

Read Revelation 5:1-14. Pictured is a scene in heaven. One from the line of David, King Jesus, is on the throne. He takes the scroll and delivers the people from their sins. All the people praise His greatness. If the Bible had stopped with David, we would all be in trouble. But it didn't. Jesus is the King of all kings. He never sinned. He never failed. He alone conquered death.

What does it mean for Jesus to be King over your life? Journal today about how the Kingship of Jesus affects your life on a daily basis. And then spend some time simply praising Jesus as the King of all kings and the Lord of all lords.

The Promised New Covenant

"This is the covenant I will make with the house of Israel after that time," declares the LORD. "I will put my law in their minds and write it on their hearts. I will be their God, and they will be my people."
Jeremiah 31:33

Many people lost their possessions in Hurricane Katrina. One of the things we lost was my wife's 1990 Toyota Camry. Two weeks after the hurricane, a church from New Mexico called me. The pastor asked if we had lost a car. I told him we had. That's when he told me that his church wanted to give us a car to replace the old one. I was at a retreat in Texas at the time. He told me to wait there so they could drive over a new car for us.

So we waited. The next day, this pastor and his youth minister drove up in an almost new GMC Yukon SUV. Leather seats. Tinted windows. Let's just say it was a lot nicer than an old 1990 Toyota Camry! We were amazed. They handed us the keys and told us we could have the car for as long as we needed it. God's provision is truly amazing!

A similar situation took place in the Old Testament. The old covenant, which we have studied up to this point, had been broken. The people of God had disobeyed Him. They had not kept their part of the covenant. But God was not giving up on them. In Jeremiah 31:31-34, God showed that His grace truly is amazing as He promises them a new covenant. This is one of the most important passages in the Old Testament, so let's dive in and see what it means for our covenant with God today.

Day 1 >

Jeremiah 31:31; Galatians 4:1-7

In this passage, Jeremiah was speaking to the Israelites during a very difficult time. They were struggling to stay alive as a nation. Soon, they would be attacked, and the whole city of Jerusalem would be destroyed. In Jeremiah 31:31, Jeremiah began to speak of a time when God would restore His people.

Read Galatians 4:1-7. These verses talk about when that time finally came. Verses 4 and 5 show that God sent Jesus to the world to complete the new covenant that Jeremiah talked about in Jeremiah 31. Jesus was the answer to the Old Testament prophecy.

Do you know anyone who is going through a difficult time? Look for an opportunity to encourage that person this week with promises from Jesus. Write down a few of the promises that might be comforting to that person and then pray for a chance to share them.

Day 2 >>

**Jeremiah 31:31-32;
Romans 9:30-33**

In Jeremiah 31:31-32, God said He was making a new covenant with the house of Israel and the house of Judah. Does that mean that this covenant doesn't apply to us? Is it just for the Jewish people of the Old Testament? Not at all.

Read Romans 9:30-33. Gentiles (which means non-Jewish people) are included in God's new covenant based on their faith in Christ. The good news of the New Testament is that these covenants between God and His chosen people in the Old Testament do not leave us out. By faith, we have the incredible, eternal privilege of being in covenant with God as His chosen people!

Write a prayer of thanks today for God's willingness to include you in His covenant. Is this something you deserve? How can you express your thanks to Him as a result of your faith in Him?

Day 3 >>>

Jeremiah 31:33; John 3:1-16

What do we mean by a "new" covenant? It was new in terms of when it was given. More importantly, it was new in terms of what it meant. Read Jeremiah 31:33, and you will see that this covenant would be written in the minds and hearts of His people. What does this mean?

Read John 3:1-16. When you enter into a relationship with God, you are born again. You start over with a new heart filled with God's love. Because Jesus' love is written on your heart, you are His child. Jeremiah

31:33 says, "I will be their God, and they will be my people."

As you journal today, write what it means to be a child of God. What does it mean for His love to be written on your heart? Pray today that God will renew your heart's desire for Him.

Day 4

Jeremiah 31:34; Hebrews 10:15-18

Yesterday, we learned that the new covenant would be written on the hearts of God's people. What does the Bible mean when it talks about God's covenant written on our hearts? Read Jeremiah 31:34. God says He will completely forgive our sins. He chooses not to even remember them!

Read Hebrews 10:15-18. What an amazing thought. The God of the universe knows everything. But He chooses to forget one thing: our sins! He does this because of His new covenant with us. Once we trust in Jesus, we don't ever have to worry about God bringing up our past sins.

Forgiveness is one of the greatest gifts of being in covenant with God. How does this gift affect your relationship with Him? Ask God to forgive any unconfessed sins today. Journal about how important God's forgiveness is in your life.

Day 5 >>>>>

Jeremiah 31:31-37;
Hebrews 6:16-20

When someone tells you they are going to do something, you want to know it is really going to happen, right? As we close this week, look back over Jeremiah 31:31-37. Circle every time you see the words "declares the Lord" in this passage.

This is God's guarantee of His new covenant with His people. Read Hebrews 6:16-20. God cannot lie. If Jeremiah 31:31-37 says God is declaring the promises of this new covenant, you can know for certain that the new covenant is totally guaranteed.

When you place your faith in God through Christ and enter into covenant with Him, He is always going to be faithful to His Word. Write some ways this affects your relationship with God. Then write a prayer asking God to continually renew your heart so that you may grow to be more faithful in keeping your promises to Him.

The Seal of the New Covenant

And you also were included in Christ when you heard the word of truth, the gospel of your salvation. Having believed, you were marked in him with a seal, the promised Holy Spirit. **Ephesians 1:13**

Last week, I told you about a church that was generous enough to give my wife and me a car after Hurricane Katrina. But the good fortune we thought we had found seemed to disappear as quickly as it appeared. As we began driving home from Texas to Georgia, a guy swerved off of the road into the side of the Yukon. Less than 24 hours after we received this new car, we got into a wreck! I called the pastor who had given us the car. He had every right to be angry. I'll never forget what he told me. He said, "Don't worry about it. We've got it covered." What an amazing response.

Remember the foundation of the "new" covenant? It's God's forgiveness. Even though we sin, even though we break our promises to God, we are forgiven because of Jesus' sacrifice on the cross. When it seems like we've completely broken covenant with God, by His grace He looks at our lives and says, "I've got it covered."

How can we be sure our sins are covered? We know because of the presence of the Holy Spirit in our lives. This week, we're going to study Ephesians 1:3-14 together to see how God seals His covenant with us. These verses contain some incredible promises. The effect of these promises on our lives is huge. Let's dive in and see what it means to have the Holy Spirit's seal in our lives.

Day 1 >

Ephesians 1:3-13;
Romans 8:28-39

Read Ephesians 1:3-13. Circle every time you see the words "chosen," "predestined," or "purpose." A lot of people get confused when they see these words. Did God really choose us? What does it mean for God to predestine us? Does God really have a set purpose for my life?

Read Romans 8:28-39. There are three important truths in this passage: God knows everything about us; God loves us; God has a plan for us. Ephesians 1:12 says that God wants us to live for the praise of His glory. Romans 8:29 tells us that we do this by becoming more like Jesus. That's the purpose of our lives: to look more and more like Jesus every day.

Journal today about God's purpose for your life. How can you look more like Jesus at the end of this week than you do now? Pray that God will conform you more and more into the image of Christ today.

Day 2 >>

Ephesians 1:3-13; Isaiah 49:14-18

Read Ephesians 1:3-13 again. Circle every time you see the words "we" or "us" mentioned. When Paul says "we" or "us," he is referring to the Jewish people. But look

at verse 13. Paul says "you." Here, he is referring to the Gentiles. Why does he change his emphasis?

The Gentiles often felt left out because they weren't Jewish. They felt like they didn't really matter in the family of God. But Paul told them loudly and clearly that just like the Jewish people, they really do matter to God!

Read Isaiah 49:14-18. Read verse 16, which says that God has engraved His people on the palms of His hands. What an incredible thought! As you journal today, think about how personal God's love for us is. How does His passion for you affect your relationship with Him? Thank God for His personal love for you as a child of His.

Day 3 >>>

Ephesians 1:13; Ephesians 4:29-32

Ephesians 1:13 tells us that when the Holy Spirit comes into our lives He is there to stay. He "seals" His presence in our lives when we place our faith in Christ.

Think about what this means. Look over at Ephesians 4:29-32. The Bible tells us that, because the Holy Spirit lives in each of us, our lives are surrendered to following His leadership. One example is in the way we act around others. We grieve the Spirit who lives in us when we don't honor Him with the way we talk about and treat others.

Journal today about how your words do or do not reflect the Spirit of God who lives in you. How can you honor the Holy Spirit with the way you act around others today? Thank God for the seal of the Holy Spirit, and pray that He will help you not to grieve the Holy Spirit with your actions.

Day 4 >>>>
Ephesians 1:14; 2 Corinthians 5:1-5

An engagement ring symbolizes the future uniting of two lives. In Ephesians 1:14, the Holy Spirit is a bit like a spiritual engagement ring. Though we may have a relationship with God, we are not yet united perfectly with Him. This will happen when we get to heaven. Until that time, the Holy Spirit is a deposit, a promise that we will one day be reunited with God.

Read 2 Corinthians 5:1-5. These verses talk about how we are longing for the day when we will be with God. When we place our faith in Christ, we're assured that we will be with Him forever. That's what God's covenant with us is all about!

Journal today about the assurance we have as Christians through the Holy Spirit. What does it mean for Him to be a "deposit" in your life? Thank God for the confidence that one day you will be in His presence in heaven forever.

covenant: Knowing God—His Relationship With His People

Ephesians 1:14;
Deuteronomy 7:6-11

Toward the end of Ephesians 1:14, it says we are God's possession. How incredible is that? You and I belong to God. We are completely His, and nothing can separate us from Him. That's how we know we will be with Him in heaven. Because we belong to Him; we belong in His presence!

Some people might think, "Since I'm sealed with the Holy Spirit and guaranteed eternity in heaven, I can live my life however I want." But that's not what covenant is all about. Read Deuteronomy 7:6-11. Here we see that God has made us His possessions. But pay close attention to verse 11. Our obedience to God is motivated by the fact that we are His possessions.

Write what it means for you to belong to God. How does this affect the way you live today? Thank God for making you His possession, and ask Him for strength to honor Him with your life.

Covenant Requirements

Then the LORD said to Moses, "Write down these words, for in accordance with these words I have made a covenant with you and with Israel." **Exodus 34:27**

How would you describe your closest friends? Something like loyal, kind, forgiving, trustworthy, and enjoyable to be around? What would happen if your friends were loyal and you weren't? If they could trust you but you couldn't trust them? Close friendships are two-way streets. Whenever these traits are present on both sides, friendship is the most fulfilling.

Up until this point in our study of covenant, we've spent most of our time focusing on God's faithfulness to us. But as we move deeper in our study of what it means to be in covenant with God, we need to examine our requirements in this relationship. We know that God initiates a covenant with us totally because of His grace, not because we earn it or deserve it. At the same time, our lives should reflect the loyalty, kindness, and forgiveness that He has shown to us.

This week, we're going to study Exodus 34:10-28. These verses show us an overview of the covenant God had with Moses and His people, which we have already studied. But this time, we're going to look at the requirements God gives for His people to keep their covenant with Him. And along the way, we'll learn more about what is expected of us as we live in covenant with God. So, let's see how to make sure that our relationship with Him is a two-way street.

covenant: Knowing God—His Relationship with His People

Day 1

Exodus 34:10; Ezekiel 36:22-23

Read Exodus 34:10. Why was God making this covenant with His people? God blessed His people so that all the nations in the world would see how awesome He is. Now read Ezekiel 36:22-23. God said that He was going to bless His people so His name would be known as great.

Think about why God initiates a covenant with us. He wants to show His power, His grace, and His mercy in our lives so that everyone around us will recognize His greatness. God's covenant with us is ultimately centered on Him, not us. That's why our obedience is so important. When we obey, we show others that God is worthy of our worship.

Journal today about how your covenant with God can be a witness to how awesome He is. How can God show His greatness through you today? Pray that God will receive glory in the covenant He has with you.

Day 2

Exodus 34:14; Deuteronomy 4:23-24

I'm pretty jealous. I don't want my wife to show love and devotion to another man. She has promised to love and devote herself to me. This doesn't mean I don't trust her or that I am envious of her. That would be unhealthy jealousy. Wanting to have all of her love is natural because we've made a total commitment to a relationship.

Read Exodus 34:14. It says God is jealous. This jealousy is very similar to the kind of jealousy I just described. God is worthy of all of our love and devotion. If we show love and devotion to other gods, Deuteronomy 4:23-24 says He is like a consuming fire. His jealousy springs from His love for His people and the worth of His character.

Write how you think God's jealousy reflects His love in your life. How does our sin keep us from giving God all of the worship that He deserves? Pray that God will be honored with your worship of Him today.

Day 3 >>>
Exodus 34:11-17; 1 Corinthians 8:4-6

As God begins to talk about His people's requirements in their covenant with Him, He commands them to avoid worshiping idols. What is an idol? An idol is anything we worship or follow, apart from God. In Exodus 34:11-17, God tells His people to break down the altars, stones, and poles that were set up to worship other gods.

Now look at 1 Corinthians 8:4-6. Those verses show us that idols should never be present in a Christian's life. Only God is worthy of our worship through Christ. We may not set up altars, stones, or poles, but that doesn't mean we aren't tempted to worship idols just like the people were in these two passages of Scripture.

What idols in your life are you tempted to worship instead of God? Journal about what you can do to get rid of those idols. Ask God for forgiveness, and confess to Him that He alone is worthy of all your worship.

Day 4 >>>>

Exodus 34:15-16; 2 Corinthians 6:14-7:1

What does it mean to be holy? Read Exodus 34:15-16. God warns His people to be separate from the nations around them. Those nations worshiped many gods, and God wanted His people to be set apart from them. That's what it means to be holy . . . to be "set apart." To be separate.

Should you stop hanging out with non-Christians? Not necessarily. But your life should be set apart for a different purpose. Read 2 Corinthians 6:14-7:1. We should avoid living our lives like those who don't worship God. When we're set apart, we'll reflect God's holiness to the people around us. That will lead them to worship God.

As you journal today, list three differences that set you apart from others around you who don't worship God. How can you stay holy in those areas of your life? Pray that God will help you to be holy so that others will see His holiness in you.

Day 5 >>>>>

**Exodus 34:24-28;
1 Corinthians 10:31**

Read Exodus 34:24-28. The requirements God gave the Israelites in their covenant with Him can be divided into two categories: things to do and things to avoid. God told His people to celebrate certain feasts and to rest on the seventh day. He also told them to both avoid coming before God empty-handed and giving sacrifices that are not pleasing to Him.

Now read 1 Corinthians 10:31. This sums up the spirit of Exodus 34:24-28. Everything we do or don't do is aimed at one purpose: glorifying God. God wants His greatness to be reflected in our lives. We may need to do or not do certain things in order for Him to be honored in our lives.

Journal today about three actions you can do to bring glory to God. Then journal about three actions you can avoid in order to bring glory to God. Ask God to use your life today to bring Him honor and praise.

Covenant Sacredness

memory verse

When they came to the threshing floor of Kidon, Uzzah reached out his hand to steady the ark, because the oxen stumbled. The LORD's anger burned against Uzzah, and he struck him down because he had put his hand on the ark. So he died there before God. **1 Chronicles 13:9-10**

How devoted are you to Christ? Are you totally sold out to Him, mostly devoted, or not very devoted at all? Isn't it OK to be devoted to God most of the time? Isn't it too much to expect 100 percent devotion to Him? Let's look at it another way.

What would you think if I said I was 95 percent committed to my wife? What if I said 5 percent of my devotion went to someone else? You would say I was a bad husband! Well, if my wife deserves 100 percent, then I'm quite sure God deserves 100 percent!

This week, we're going to learn that total commitment to God is necessary in our relationship with Him. Remember, we are not just focusing on God's faithfulness to us but on our faithfulness to Him. God's faithfulness to us is always 100 percent. The question we'll ask this week is "Are we being totally obedient to Him?"

The passage we'll study is from 1 Chronicles 13. It's a stunning story about a man named Uzzah who experienced a shocking consequence because He did not obey God completely. This story is a good reminder that our God is worthy of our complete devotion. (As you read this story, thank God that we have the opportunity to be forgiven of our sins through what Jesus did on the cross.) Let's see what that kind of devotion is all about.

Day 1 >

1 Chronicles 13:1-6;
1 Corinthians 6:18-20

In order to understand 1 Chronicles 13:1-6, we need to know more about the ark. Basically, the ark was the most holy object in the people's worship because it symbolized God's presence among them. Read Exodus 25:10-22 for some context.

Now read 1 Corinthians 6:18-20. This passage teaches us that our bodies are the Holy Spirit's temple. We don't have an ark that symbolizes God's presence. We have God living inside us! In biblical times, there were rules and regulations on how the people of God should honor His holiness by the way they handled the ark. Today we honor God's holiness by the way we live.

Journal today about what it means to have God living in you. How does this affect your life? Ask God to help you honor His holiness today by the way you live.

Day 2 >>

1 Chronicles 13:7-8;
Psalm 145:1-7

Celebration. This is the word that describes the mood in 1 Chronicles 13:7-8. And they had reason to celebrate. The Philistines had captured the ark in a battle many years before. Since then, the ark hadn't been central to the Israelite's worship. When the symbol of the presence of God in their lives was back, they immediately began to celebrate "with all their might before God."

Celebration is a natural response to the presence of God in our lives. Read Psalm 145:1-7. This is a prayer of celebration. And remember, this passage is from the Old Testament. Those people didn't have the Holy Spirit living in them, which, as we know, guarantees the presence of God in our lives forever. How much more do we have reason to celebrate today?

As you journal today, write out a prayer of celebration, much like Psalm 145, that praises God for the joy of His presence. Then think about how you can celebrate His presence during your day.

Day 3
1 Chronicles 13:9-11; Numbers 4:15

Read 1 Chronicles 13:9-11. At first glance, it seems like this guy, Uzzah, was doing a good thing. But God had established guidelines for handling the ark. Read Numbers 4:15, and compare it to 1 Chronicles 13:9-11. See if you can notice what Uzzah did wrong.

In the first place, the ark should have never been on a cart (see 1 Chronicles 13:7). Numbers 4:15 says that certain people were supposed to carry the ark and they were not to touch the holy things. If anyone touched the ark they would die. Uzzah had completely ignored God's commands for how to handle the ark. As a result, he lost his life.

Why is it important to know God's commands in order to obey Him? Record your thoughts. What changes do you need to make to be totally obedient to God? Pray that God will help you to make those changes so that you will honor His holiness with your life.

Day 4 >>>>
1 Chronicles 13:9-11;
Romans 12:1

The sin of Uzzah in 1 Chronicles 13 was basically a worship issue. The ark was at the center of the Israelites' worship. God had given commands for how He was to be worshiped. Uzzah broke those commands.

The New Testament gives us commands for worship today. Read Romans 12:1. This verse shows us the three main characteristics of true worship. First, worship is a living sacrifice. Worship is a lot more than what we do on Sunday mornings or Wednesday nights at church; worship is about a lifestyle. Second, worship is holy. That means we worship God with our purity each and every day. And finally, worship is pleasing to God. Is your worship a living sacrifice? Is your life pure and holy? Is your life pleasing to God? Write how you can change certain

areas of your life to be a better worshiper. Pray that God will receive true worship from your life today.

Day 5 >>>>>

1 Chronicles 13:11-14; Romans 12:2

David was pretty upset in 1 Chronicles 13. (Read 1 Chronicles 15:13, and you'll see that he realized they had disobeyed God's commands.) So David put the ark in Obed-Edom's house. Look at what happened in verse 14. The Lord's blessing was all over this guy! Why? Because the presence of God was at the center of his house.

Read Romans 12:2. This verse teaches that when the presence of God is at the center of our lives, we will know and experience God's will. God's will for our lives involves blessing and satisfaction. We will experience total satisfaction only when we worship God with total obedience.

Journal today about your desire for total satisfaction. Do you want to be completely satisfied in this life? How can total obedience bring total satisfaction? Pray that God will show His blessing in your life today as you live in total obedience to Him.

God's Covenant Faithfulness

"This is what the LORD says: 'If you can break my covenant with the day and my covenant with the night, so that day and night no longer come at their appointed time, then my covenant with David my servant—and my covenant with the Levites who are priests ministering before me—can be broken and David will no longer have a descendant to reign on his throne.'" **Jeremiah 33:20-21**

A lot of people in the world think the Bible is just a book. Many people don't believe it has authority in their lives. But the Bible isn't just one good book among many. Instead, it's completely unique. It alone is totally inspired by God. One of the many reasons we know this is because of the Bible's prophecies.

A prophet's job was to take the Word of God and deliver it to His people. Many times, the message addressed both the situation going on in the prophet's lifetime and that which was going to happen in the future. Examples exist throughout Scripture of prophecies that would end up coming true hundreds of years later. These prophecies not only show us how unique the Bible is, but they also show that God is always faithful to His promises.

In Jeremiah 33:14-26, God promised to bring salvation to His people through King David's line. This was a promise that Jesus was coming one day. Now, if God was faithful to come through on the greatest promise He made in history, then we can be sure of this: He will be faithful to come through on all of His promises in our life today. Let's take a journey to see God's faithfulness all over the pages of this book.

Day 1 >

Jeremiah 33:14; Jeremiah 23:5-8

Jeremiah was prophesying during a very difficult time for God's people. The city of Jerusalem would soon be destroyed. The Israelites would be taken from their homes and their families. They would soon be slaves in another land. Things were not going well!

But 13 times, Jeremiah said, "days are coming . . ." Whenever Jeremiah said these words, he gave a promise from God about what God was going to do in the future. Read Jeremiah 23:5-8. Jeremiah reminded the people of God that one day God was going to restore them. As Jeremiah 33:14 says, one day God is going to fulfill His promises of grace to them.

Journal today about the importance of God's promises when we go through difficult times. How do these promises give us strength and hope? Thank God for His constant faithfulness to us.

Day 2 >>

Jeremiah 33:15-16; John 8:42-47

Jeremiah 33:15-16 mentions a "righteous Branch," a King who will do what is just and right. Verse 16 says He will be called "The Lord Our Righteousness." Three times, Jeremiah mentions the promised righteousness of the King.

Now read John 8:42-47. Jesus said that, contrary to the devil who is the father of lies, He has never once sinned. He asked the religious leaders if they had any evidence that He had sinned . . . any evidence at all . . . even one little time. They didn't have an answer. That's because Jesus was completely righteous, just like Jeremiah 33 prophesied. He is set apart among all people in history because He never sinned . . . not even once.

Write why you think the sinlessness of Jesus is so important? Could He have died for our sins if He had sinned himself? Journal today about how His sinlessness helps us when we are tempted to sin.

Day 3 >>>

Jeremiah 33:15-16; Luke 19:1-10

Jeremiah 33:16 says that "Judah" (another name for the people of God) would one day be saved through this righteous King. This was a promise that one day the Israelites would not be slaves in a foreign land. But it was more. It was also a promise that the people would no longer be slaves to sin. Jesus would completely redeem them from their sin.

Read the story of Jesus and Zacchaeus in Luke 19:1-10. Zacchaeus was a tax collector, which was considered a pretty detestable job. People were shocked when Jesus went and had dinner with him. But look at verse 10. It describes the whole purpose of Jesus coming to the earth. He had come to bring salvation to even the most detestable sinners.

What does "salvation" really mean to you? Think about what it means to be "saved." Record your thoughts. Thank God for saving you, and ask God to help you understand more and more what it means to be saved from your sin.

Day 4 >>>>
Jeremiah 33:15-16; John 14:25-27

We have seen that Jesus was completely righteous and that He would bring salvation. Read verse 16 again. It says that the people of Jerusalem would live in safety. To a people living in a dangerous time, this was an incredible promise!

People fear a variety of things. The disciples were no different. Read what Jesus said to them in John 14:25-27. He told them that He came to give them peace, total peace. This would mean that they would never have to fear anything. They wouldn't even have to fear death. Why? Because Jesus had conquered the ultimate fear that we might face. As a result, He had fulfilled God's promise to bring complete safety to His people. Journal today about any fears you may have in your life. How does Jesus bring safety in the middle of those fears? Thank God for the peace and security He has promised to us through Christ.

Day 5 >>>>>

**Jeremiah 33:17-26;
Revelation 19:11-16**

Read Jeremiah 33:17-26. These verses are all about God's faithfulness to His promises. After the two verses that describe the coming of Christ in the future, God spends eight verses describing how He is going to be completely faithful to that promise. Just as sure as the sun rises and sets, God's faithfulness is guaranteed.

Now read Revelation 19:11-16. These verses talk about Jesus' return. Notice that His name will be called "Faithful and True." The King of kings and the Lord of lords is going to show the world that God is completely faithful to every single one of His promises.

Journal today about the impact of God's faithfulness in your life. Is He worthy of all your trust? If so, how can you trust Him more with your life today? Pray that God will increase your faith so that you will trust in Him completely with your life.

Covenant Blessings and Consequences

"I will look on you with favor and make you fruitful and increase your numbers, and I will keep my covenant with you." **Leviticus 26:9**

I recently spent some time in Sudan, Africa, where Muslim-run armies have killed millions of Sudanese over the last 20 years, many of them Christians. The Church in Sudan has experienced great poverty, suffering, and destruction through civil war.

The evidence of war was everywhere. Bombed buildings and churches were scattered throughout the African bush. People lived in makeshift homes. As I talked with Sudanese Christians, I expressed my sympathy. But every time I did this, they would repeat the Sudanese Christians' favorite saying: "God is greater." They believe God is greater than any sufferings or any pain they may experience.

We need to remember something: Just because we experience pain, suffering, or hardship in our lives, that does not mean God is punishing us. Suffering is not a direct result of our individual disobedience to God. The suffering of the Sudanese was a result of their obedience to God.

This week, we will see God promise to bless those who are faithful to Him and curse those who are unfaithful to Him. This doesn't mean that if we experience hard times, God is cursing us. It means blessings and consequences go along with our obedience or disobedience to God. Let's read Leviticus 26 and discover the God of the covenant who is greater than anything in this world.

Day 1 >

Leviticus 26:9; Matthew 24:32-35

As we have been studying what it means to be in covenant with God, we have seen in Scripture that God is completely trustworthy when it comes to His promises. That's exactly what He's saying in Leviticus 26:9. This week, we're going to see several sides of God's loyalty.

God is faithful in blessing His people when they are faithful to Him. God is equally faithful to withdraw His blessing from His people when they aren't true to Him. However, God restores His disobedient people. His covenant with them is never completely broken. Regardless of the situation, God's Word is always faithful. Read Matthew 24:32-35 to see Jesus' teaching.

As we begin this week, journal your thoughts on how God shows His faithfulness when we are both obedient and disobedient. Pray that God will help you to understand the blessings and the consequences that are involved in being in covenant with Him.

Day 2 >>

Leviticus 26:10-13; Psalm 1

Read Leviticus 26:10-13. God promises blessings to the faithful. Now read Psalm 1. God blesses His people so they may know His presence, provision, and protection.

You may be thinking, "What about those people in Sudan? God didn't protect and provide for them."

At this point, we need to remember that God's promises are eternal. Many of the Sudanese have died in this difficult time. But remember that those Christians who died were completely protected from spiritual death and now find themselves in heaven with God. Those who are left have known God's presence in incredible ways over the last 20 years. God is all about blessing the faithful!

Journal about a few ways God has blessed your faithfulness to Him. How has God's blessing been evident in your life even in difficult times? Pray that God will make you more faithful to Him so that you can experience more of His blessings in your life.

Day 3 >>>
Leviticus 26:14-20; Deuteronomy 27:14-26

We've seen the good news. Here's the bad news: God blesses the faithful, but He disciplines the unfaithful. Read Leviticus 26:14-20. See how God promises to bring serious consequences to those who disobey? Now read Deuteronomy 27:14-26. Notice the curses that come as a result of sin.

We have a tendency to take sin lightly. We don't always think it's that big of a deal. We justify our sins. We think God won't care too much if we disobey Him just a little. We continue committing particular sins, almost like it doesn't matter that much to God. But these verses give us a very different picture. God is extremely serious about sin, and there are always consequences.

Journal today about areas of your life in which you have become casual with sin. How do you think God views sin in your life? Confess those sins today to God, and then ask Him to help you see sin as He sees it.

Day 4 >>>>

Leviticus 26:40-45; 1 John 1:8-10

God blesses the faithful, and He disciplines the unfaithful. But if those are the only two characteristics of God, then we're in a lot of trouble. We are all unfaithful to God in some way! As a result, we deserve His punishment. But the third characteristic of God we see in this chapter is that God restores those who repent of their sin. See God's promise in Leviticus 26:40-45.

Read 1 John 1:8-10. When we see our sin the way God sees it, when we express our sorrow to Him for our sin and then turn from it, God is ready to forgive us and to give us a new start. And this is possible only through what Jesus did on the cross for us. What does it mean to be cleansed from unrighteousness? What do you need to repent of today to experience His forgiveness? Spend time today praising God for His faithfulness to restore your life even when you have sinned against Him.

Day 5 >>>>>

Leviticus 26:12; Jeremiah 24:7

Read Leviticus 26:12. This is a common phrase we see repeated in the Old Testament. Another example is in Jeremiah 24:7. God promises that when His people are in covenant with Him, He will walk among them, and they will serve Him with all their hearts.

Christians all around the world are experiencing suffering and persecution for their faith. But God is faithful to be with His people and to bless them as they follow Him. Even though our brothers and sisters in Sudan have experienced very difficult times, they have remained faithful to God. As a result, they have seen His faithfulness to them.

Take time to write a prayer for God's faithfulness for all of those who are undergoing persecution because of His name. Pray that God will show His presence, His provision, and His promises to them even in the middle of their suffering.

Covenant Reneged

He who forms the mountains, creates the wind, and reveals his thoughts to man, he who turns dawn to darkness, and treads the high places of the earth—the LORD God Almighty is his name. **Amos 4:13**

We had a basketball goal outside our garage at the house where I grew up, and the garage door had windows all the way across it. I can still hear my dad's voice: "Make sure to put the garage door up." That way, we would avoid breaking a window. And we obeyed Dad. Most of the time.

I was shooting baskets by myself one day. I didn't see a reason to put the garage door up; I wasn't going to miss. So I shot around for a while. But before I knew it, the sound of shattered glass filled the air. Now, I knew there would be consequences to my disobedience! Did that mean my dad didn't love me? Was it wrong for him to be disappointed? Was it wrong for him to discipline me? Absolutely not. His disappointment was the right response.

In Amos 4, we see a side of God we don't often talk about. Throughout this passage, we're going to observe God's wrath coming down on His people because of their disobedience. Does this mean God didn't love them? Was it wrong for Him to be disappointed? Was it wrong for Him to discipline His children? Absolutely not. God's response to His people's disobedience was completely right. In no way did it conflict with His love for them. This week, we'll see the image of a holy God who loves His people enough to discipline them. We'll learn how he does the same thing with us today.

Amos 4:2; Psalm 89:35-37

Amos was a prophet who lived during a very prosperous time for God's people. Things seemed to be going really well for the Israelites. But the people had become unfaithful to God. Amos warned them of God's coming judgment.

Amos 4:2 says that God has sworn these things by His holiness. Read Psalm 89:35. God used the same words right before He made a promise. This is another way of saying, "Mark it down. What I'm about to say is undoubtedly going to happen." After Amos said this, he gave a description of God's judgment. In the years that would follow, everything would come true. The nation of Israel and then the nation of Judah would both be destroyed. The people would experience the discipline of God.

In your journal, answer this question: Because God is holy, does that mean He must discipline His people? Pray today that God will help you understand His discipline more this week.

Amos 4:4; Numbers 14:5-12

How do you define sin? Read Amos 4:4. Here, God talks about the people's sins. The literal meaning of this word is rebellion. The people of God had rebelled

against Him, turned away from Him and chosen to do what they wanted to.

Read Numbers 14:5-12. Here, you'll see another example of the rebelliousness of the children of God. The people had a choice: they either could trust God and go into the Promised Land, or they could rebel against God and stay where they were. They rebelled, and, as a result, they experienced the discipline of God by wandering in a desert for 40 years.

Journal today about sins that you are struggling with or have struggled with. Can you identify rebellion against God at the root of those sins? How can you get rid of this rebellion? Pray today that God will increase your desire to honor Him by avoiding sin in your life.

Day 3 >>>

Amos 4:1-5; Matthew 22:37-38

These verses can be difficult to understand. It helps to know some background. For example, Bethel and Gilgal were two cities known for their idolatry; many people worshiped different gods in those places. But don't miss it; verses 4-5 say that God was being worshiped in those places, too.

So there's the problem. The people of God were worshiping Him while they also worshiped foreign gods. They had split their devotion among many different gods.

But that was not true worship. Read Matthew 22:37-38. True worship is loving the one true God with everything you have. We can't worship God and follow other gods. He demands and deserves all of our love and worship.

Are you like the people in Amos 4? What are the other "gods" that compete for your worship? Journal today about how your devotion can get caught up in other things. Then express your desire to give God all of your heart in worship to Him.

Day 4
Amos 4:1-5; Matthew 22:39-40

Do you remember how we said the people of God were really prosperous during this time? Many of them had become rich. They had everything they wanted. But in gaining wealth, they had oppressed the poor and crushed the needy. They had not shown God's love through properly using the wealth He had given them.

Read Matthew 22, paying attention to verses 39-40. Jesus said that, in addition to love for God, we must also love each other. The people in Amos' day had completely ignored this part of the commandment. They had satisfied their own desires with their money, but they had not paid any attention to the poor.

If you live in the United States, you are wealthy compared to the majority of people in the world. Journal today about how you can use the money or possessions you have to help someone who has less than you. Pray for an opportunity to honor God with your possessions today.

Day 5 >>>>>

Amos 4:6-13; Hebrews 12:4-13

Read Amos 4:6-13. Notice that God disciplined His people to bring them back to Himself. But over and over again, His people resisted God's discipline and continued to sin. As you come to the end of the passage, the message is clear: God's people cannot experience satisfaction apart from complete trust and obedience in Him.

Read Hebrews 12:4-13. God's discipline is a demonstration of His love. These verses talk about our Heavenly Father's discipline for His children, whom He loves greatly. The Bible encourages us not to ignore God's discipline but to receive it and let it bring us back to Him.

As we close out this week, journal about how you have seen God's discipline in your life. How have you responded? Have you allowed His discipline to bring you back to Him? Pray that God will help you to recognize and respond to His discipline in your life as a sign of His love for you.

The Choice

This is what the LORD says to the house of Israel: "Seek me and live." **Amos 5:4**

Make a priority list in the blanks below. In the first blank, list the number one priority in your life. Be honest. Then put your second priority down, then your third, and so on.

1.

2.

3.

4.

5.

God's people had divided their devotion. In Amos 5:4-15, God told His people they needed to make a choice. Either they could follow Him, or they could follow the other gods. They could not do both.

Look back at your list. If you have God on there, cross Him off. Instead of thinking about God on your priority list, I want you to start thinking about God as the paper you write your priority list on. This changes everything about how we love and worship God. Most of us are content to have God as a part of our lives—even as the number one part of our lives. But nowhere in Scripture does God ask to be a "part" of our lives. Instead, God is our life. He is our everything.

As we study this passage from Amos 5, don't forget that these people had a choice: Either seek God in every part of their lives, or continue to keep Him as only one aspect of their lives. One choice leads to life, one to death. We have the same choice in our lives, as well. Let's take a closer look.

Day 1 >

Amos 5:5-6; Isaiah 1:10-17

Read Amos 5:5-6. God warned His people not to seek Bethel. Why? Bethel was a place to worship God. But the people had lost sight of what true worship is about: obedience.

Read Isaiah 1:10-17. Here, Isaiah tells God's people their offerings are meaningless if they are not obeying God. We may not give sacrifices today, but the same principle is true for us. We can get so busy "doing" church that we completely miss out on what it means to seek God by obeying Him. God may be telling you and me, "Don't seek your religion; seek me!"

Journal today about what it means to seek God. Do you ever get so busy doing church activities that you begin to miss out on simply seeking God's face? Pray that He will teach you this week what it means to seek Him with all your heart.

Day 2 >>

Amos 5:7-13; Jeremiah 5:26-28

In Amos 5:7-13, we once again see God disciplining His people because of the way they treated the poor. When God said they had turned justice into bitterness, He was talking about how they had disobeyed God's law by not having concern for other people. When that happened, Amos said, they were committing acts of unrighteousness. Their sin was dishonoring God.

Read Jeremiah 5:26-28. Those verses describe the failure of God's people to defend the rights of the poor. This is what the people in Amos' day had failed to do. They had grown so happy and content with what they had that they didn't show concern for those who were needy.

Journal today about one practical way that you can show concern for someone who is needy this week. After you've journaled, pray for the needy person that you are going to help, and then obey God's command by putting your concern into action.

Day 3
Amos 5:8-9; Psalm 104

Read Amos 5:8-9. You probably have parentheses around verses 8-9 in your Bible. In the middle of this description of God's discipline of His people, God reminded His people of who He is. He reminded them that He is Lord over all creation, and that meant He was Lord over their lives. Everything that happened to them was in His hands.

The same thing is true for you and me today. God is in control of everything that happens in all of the universe, including everything that happens in our lives. As a result, when He speaks, we should definitely listen! God holds our lives in His hands, and we would be wise to listen to everything He says.

Before you journal today, read Psalm 104 as a prayer to God. Then journal about what it means for God to be Lord over everything in all of creation, including your life. How does this affect your relationship with Him?

Day 4 >>>>
Amos 5:14-15; Psalm 34:1-10

God commanded His people to seek good. This is the third time in Amos that God told His people to seek Him and His goodness. (See verses 4-6.) Seeking God means turning to Him, putting our confidence in Him. In other words, when we seek God, we trust Him completely.

Look over in Psalm 34:1-10. In verse 4, David said that he sought the Lord. What was the result? God answered him. In other words, when David sought God, he trusted Him. The result was that God showed Himself trustworthy. The rest of the verses after verse 4 give us a picture of how God brings blessing to those who seek Him.

Journal today about any areas of your life where you are not trusting God completely. How can you seek God more

in those areas of your life? Pray that God will help you to trust Him today with every part of your life.

Day 5 >>>>>
Amos 5:14-15; Micah 5:7-9

As we close out our week in Amos 5, notice that God not only gave His people a command, but He also gave them a promise. We saw the command yesterday. God told His people to seek Him. But don't miss the promise: "Seek good, not evil, that you may live." God said they would live because He would be with them and show mercy to them when they sought Him.

Now look at Micah 5:7-9. (Hint: Micah is three books to your right from Amos.) These verses talk about how, when God's people returned to Him, He would bless them so that they would triumph over their enemies. Those who seek God will see the benefits of God's blessings in their lives.Write down five benefits of seeking God. How can you obey Him in order to experience these benefits in your life today?

The Promise

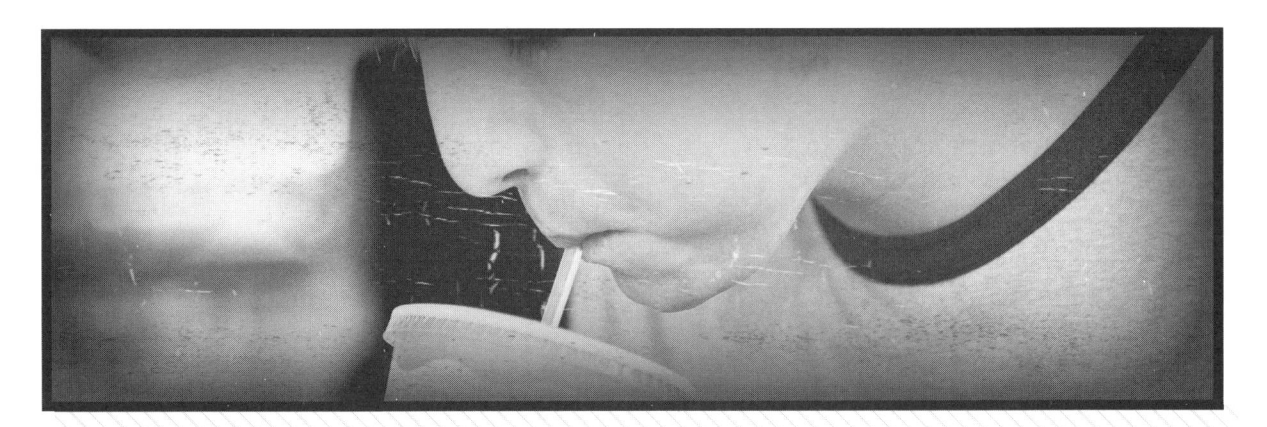

"The LORD your God is with you, he is mighty to save. He will take great delight in you, he will quiet you with his love, he will rejoice over you with singing."
Zephaniah 3:17

When you remember God's wrath and discipline, the words contained in Zephaniah 3:17 are amazing. Listen to what God says to His people through Zephaniah: "The LORD your God is with you, he is mighty to save. He will take great delight in you, he will quiet you with his love, he will rejoice over you with singing."

These words give us an incredible picture of God's love for His people, even when they had sinned against Him. Five promises for the people of God are in this one verse: God promises to be with His people, to save His people, to delight in His people, to quiet His people with His love, and to rejoice over His people. Can you imagine all of this? What amazing love from God!

God is totally willing to completely restore and renew His people when they turn back to Him. This truth is not just for the people of God in the Old Testament; it is also for us today. When we wander from God and disobey His commands, He does not give up on us. He will discipline our disobedience. But, He is always willing to renew our hearts and show us His great love so that we are brought back into intimacy with Him. Let's see how this is foretold in Zephaniah 3:9-20.

Day 1 »

Zephaniah 3:9-10; Ephesians 4:1-6

At this point in Scripture, the people of God are scattered because of their disobedience to God. This is known as the "exile" of God's people. But read Zephaniah 3:9-10. It says that one day the people will be purified of their sin and they will serve God shoulder to shoulder. Notice how, when God's people become pure, they also become unified.

Read Ephesians 4:1-6. These verses talk about the unity of the church. But as you read the rest of Ephesians, you'll notice that unity comes only when the people of God are committed to purity. This is important for us to understand. In your church or in your youth group, God desires for you to be unified.

Would you say that your church or youth group is characterized by unity or division? Journal today about how purity and holiness could bring your youth group closer together. Pray that God will use you to bring unity among His people.

Day 2 »»

Zephaniah 3:11-13; 1 Peter 5:5-7

Pride is the attitude of the heart that says, "I am in control." Pride is a big cause of sin. Read Zephaniah 3:11-13. Note that God removes those who rejoice in their pride. He replaces them with the meek

and humble, people who say in their hearts, "God is in control, and I trust Him with everything in my life."

When we are prideful, we think we're in control and have nothing to fear. But remember from Genesis 3 that fear is a direct result of our sin. Read the end of Zephaniah 3:13. When we are humble, we truly have nothing to fear. It's the same thing 1 Peter 5:5-7 teaches us. When we are humble, God will lift us up so that we have nothing to fear.

Answer this question in your journal: How does pride keep you from growing in your relationship with God? Pray that God will cleanse you of pride and give you greater humility.

Day 3 >>>

Zephaniah 3:14-17; Matthew 28:20

Do you really believe that God is with you wherever you go? I hope the answer is yes, but in order for us to answer this question honestly, we may need to turn to Scripture.

Three times in Zephaniah 3 God reminds His people that He is with them (vv. 5, 15, and 17). Jesus says the same thing to His disciples in Matthew 28:20. Scripture is clear: God is always with His people. The question remains: "Do we really believe that He is with us wherever we go today?"

Answer the question in your journal.

Ask God to make you more aware of His presence in your life today. Then journal about how knowing that God is with you changes the way you live. How does God's presence affect the way you talk, act, date, and so on?

Day 4 >>>>

Zephaniah 3:18-19; Psalm 73

As Christians, we may look at non-Christians and ask why they are doing better than we are. Maybe they have more money. Maybe they seem more popular. Maybe they seem more successful. We might ask, "Why are they doing so well when they're not trusting or following God?"

Read Zephaniah 3:18-19. God's people were asking these questions. But God reminded them that He will ultimately bring justice. Read Psalm 73, and see how the writer is struggling with this line of thinking. Look at his conclusion in the last verse. After all of his struggles, he says, "But as for me, it is good to be near God."

Why is it better to be near God than to have success in the eyes of the world? Is success about having the things of the world or about being near God? Pray that God will help you to trust Him completely with your life.

Day 5 >>>>>>

Zephaniah 3:20; Psalm 96

Picking up where we left off yesterday, Zephaniah 3:20 teaches that God will give His people honor and praise among all the nations of the earth. Satan may cause us to envy what other people in the world have. But in the end, God will save His people. We will be a testimony to everyone else that it truly is good to be near God.

Read Psalm 96. In these verses, God commands His people to tell the nations about His glory. This week, we have seen a beautiful picture of God's desire to restore and renew His people. But don't forget God's motive. He not only wants to restore us, but He also wants our renewed lives to be reflections of His glory and His love to those around us.

Write the name of one person whom you can share God's love with today. Pray for an opportunity to share with that person about what God has done to renew your heart and change your life.

The Restoration

"This is what I covenanted with you when you came out of Egypt. And my Spirit remains among you. Do not fear." **Haggai 2:5**

The manufacturers of one popular water bottle claim it cannot be broken. If one breaks, they promise to replace it for free. I have seen students doing everything they can to break them. Occasionally, these water bottles crack, but most often they survive.

The Old Testament people thought the temple was invincible. It was the place God dwelled. It was the symbol of the covenant. When the people broke this covenant, God brought discipline on them. Part of His discipline was evident when other nations attacked Jerusalem and destroyed the Temple.

After years of exile, some of God's people returned to Him. When they arrived in Jerusalem they began to rebuild the temple. But it wasn't the same. The people were depressed. Could God's glory really dwell among His people in this new Temple?

In Haggai 2:1-9, Haggai reminded the people of God's glory. These verses paint a picture of the glory of Jesus, the promised Messiah who would fully bring God's glory to His people. Let's study this passage together this week and see the foundation for what the Bible calls an unshakeable Kingdom.

Day 1 >

Haggai 2:1-3; Ezra 9:8-9

At Thanksgiving, we have a huge meal, and there are always a lot of leftovers. The remnant of the Thanksgiving meals is still there for many days! Read Haggai 2:1-3. This prophecy is addressed to the remnant of the people of Israel. Many of the Israelites had turned away and followed false gods. But the group that repented of their sins and trusted God is known as the remnant of Israel in the Old Testament.

Read Ezra 9:8-9. The book of Ezra talks about how the people of God rebuilt the temple after the exile. The idea of a "remnant" is a reminder that even when we are disobedient to God, if we repent and return to Him, He is faithful to restore us.

Journal today about a time when God restored you after disobedience in your relationship with Him. How did you see God's love and faithfulness to you during that time? Write a praise to God for His grace.

Day 2 >>

Haggai 2:4-5; Joshua 1:6-9

Read both Haggai 2:4-5 and Joshua 1:6-9. In both situations, the people of God were feeling weak. In Haggai's day, the people were weak because of the slavery they'd

experienced and because they were trying to rebuild the Temple. In Joshua's day, the people were weak because they'd wandered in the desert for 40 years.

Notice in both of these passages what God tells them is the source of their strength. Two times in these verses in Haggai, God tells them that He is with them. Joshua 1:9 says to be strong because the Lord is with you wherever you go. The Bible is showing something to us very clearly: The presence of God is the source of strength in our Christian lives.

Write today about the strength you find in the presence of God. How does His strength give you courage when you are weak? Trust God to give you strength today in His presence for any trial or temptation you may face.

Day 3 >>>
Haggai 2:6-7; Hebrews 12:25-29

Read Haggai 2:6-7. The people of God had lost confidence. But God told them He was going to shake the heavens and the earth, that He was going to bring His glory to the Temple! Now read Hebrews 12:25-29. The author quotes Haggai to show that, as God's people, we are part of an unshakeable Kingdom.

When we sin, we're tempted to think that God could never restore us completely.

There are definitely consequences to our sin. But when God restores us, He restores us completely. He gives us a new devotion to Him—all because of His grace. When we trust in Him, we can't be shaken!

List some times you have struggled in your faith. How has God shown His unchanging faithfulness to you? Write about how God has restored you, and then thank Him for the confidence that we are part of a Kingdom that won't be shaken for all of eternity.

Day 4 >>>>

Haggai 2:8; 2 Corinthians 8:8-9

As a result of their exile, God's people had lost all of their wealth. The nations around them were much more powerful. But read Haggai 2:8. God told them that all the silver and gold in the world belongs to Him. As a result, His people never needed to worry about not having what they needed.

Read 2 Corinthians 8:8-9. Remember that Jesus was God in the flesh. All the power of God belongs to Jesus. But 2 Corinthians 8 tells us that, for our sake, Jesus became poor in order that we might become rich. Through Christ, we become rich with the satisfaction that He alone can bring us.

As you journal today, list a few different ways Jesus has turned your poverty into riches. Think about ways He has turned your life around to bring you the satisfaction that comes in God alone. Then thank Christ for becoming poor so that you might become rich through Him.

Day 5 >>>>>>

Haggai 2:9; Matthew 12:6

Read Haggai 2:9. This verse helps us to realize that Haggai is talking about more than just a building. Read Matthew 12:6. In that verse, Jesus told the religious leaders that one greater than the temple was there. He was referring to Himself.

The Temple was the place where the glory of God dwelled. Haggai prophesied about a day when God Himself would dwell on earth. This is exactly what He did in Jesus. Now the presence of Christ dwells in each of us. The glory of the temple of the Holy Spirit (our bodies!) is most definitely greater than the glory of a building made by human hands.

Journal about how God shows His glory through our bodies as the temple of His Holy Spirit. How is this greater than when His glory dwelled in a building made by human hands? Pray that God will show His glory through you today in whatever you do.

God's Covenant Love

memory verse

"Know therefore that the LORD your God is God; he is the faithful God, keeping his covenant of love to a thousand generations of those who love him and keep his commands." **Deuteronomy 7:9**

What makes Christianity different from other religions? Jesus, right? No other religion has at its center a man who claimed to be sent from God, who was crucified and died, then rose from the dead, and ultimately ascended into heaven. Christianity is truly unique in this sense. And how do we account for Jesus? John 3:16 sums it up. "For God so loved . . ." In His love for us, God sent Jesus to save everyone from their sins.

The passage of Scripture we'll look at this week is another example of how Christianity is set apart from all other world religions. God doesn't sit back and wait for us to make our way to Him. God chooses to come to where we are. Instead of waiting for us to earn His love, He pursues us with His love. He comes to you and me and says, "I have made a way for you to know Me and enjoy Me."

This week, we're going to journey into Deuteronomy 7:6-13 and see God's covenant love for His people. And along the way, we'll see how His covenant love for the people of Israel in the Old Testament is a reflection of His covenant love for you and me today.

Day 1 >

Deuteronomy 7:6; 1 Peter 2:9-10

Read Deuteronomy 7:6. As God spoke to His people in this passage, He told them He had chosen them. This is what grace is all about. Grace means that God takes all the initiative to reach out and love you and me. It's important to remember that the Israelites had not earned their way to God. He had chosen to love them and pour out His blessings on them.

Read 1 Peter 2:9-10. We are a chosen people, loved by God, and created to declare His praises. When we understand that God has chosen us by His grace, our natural response will be to love Him, to give glory to His Name, and to tell others about His grace.

As you journal today, write some of the ways you have seen God's grace in your life. Then spend some time praising Him because He has chosen to love you!

Day 2 >>

Deuteronomy 7:6; Titus 2:11-14

Think about some of your most valuable possessions. Most often, these are things you buy or someone else buys for you. These possessions don't belong to anyone else. Read Deuteronomy 7:6. What do you think it means to be God's possession? Being God's possession means we belong to Him! He has bought us for a price.

Read Titus 2:11-14. In verse 14, you'll see that God "redeems" us. This word literally means He "pays the price" for us. God sent His Son, Jesus, to die on the cross for you and me so that we could belong to Him and be His possession.

Write what you think it means to be God's treasured possession. How does this make you feel? How does this affect the way you live? Memorize Deuteronomy 7:9, and then spend time today thanking Jesus for the price He paid so that you could belong to God.

Day 3 >>>
Deuteronomy 7:7-8; 1 Corinthians 1:26-31

Why did God choose to love His people? Was it because of how great they were? Was it because they were smart or powerful? Read Deuteronomy 7:7-8. The Bible says they weren't any of these things. In fact, they were a small group of people who weren't even well-respected among the other nations.

God chooses to love people who are the least likely to be loved. Read 1 Corinthians 1:26-31. These verses tell us that God chooses the foolish things of the world, the despised things, the "things that are not." This is not a pretty description of God's people! But that's the point. God's people become great because of the love of God.

Many times, we forget that we don't deserve the love God has chosen to pour out on us. As you journal today, confess your need for God's love. Admit to Him how you fall short of earning His love, and then thank Him for His forgiveness and His grace.

Day 4 >>>>
Deuteronomy 7:9-11; 1 Peter 2:4-5

We know that God's grace and love are the foundations for this covenant. But read Deuteronomy 7:9-11. While God's affection doesn't rest on our obedience, He does call us to obey His commands.

Read 1 Peter 2:4-5. Once again, these verses talk about how we're chosen by God. But then in verse 5, the Bible says we are a holy priesthood, offering our lives to God as a sacrifice of praise. When we realize we belong to God, it changes the way we live. We are holy, set apart by Him. When we realize how much He loves us, we want to honor Him through our holy living.

As you journal today, search your heart and your life to see if there are any areas that are not holy. Think about your actions, your words, your motives, and your relationships. Are they holy? Then pray that God would make you more holy today so that His holiness can be seen through your life.

Day 5 >>>>>>

Deuteronomy 7:12-13;
Psalm 107:31-38

Read Deuteronomy 7:12-13. Here we see God's promise to His people. We already know that God pours out His love on us—not because we deserve it but because of His grace. And we know our responsibility is to obey Him because we belong to Him. But now we see God's promise to bless His people as they continue to obey Him.

Read Psalm 107:31-38. These passages talk about how God's people experience His blessings as they walk in a relationship with Him. Isn't this an incredible thought?

Journal today about the blessings of God you have seen in your life this week. How has God been faithful to you? As you finish the week, spend some time in prayer simply thanking God for His blessings and expressing your desire to walk more closely with Him every day.

Evidence of God's Love

"Give thanks to the Lord of lords: His love endures forever. to him who alone does great wonders, His love endures forever."

Psalm 136:3-4

Thinks about what it's like at a game when your team scores. You probably don't sit there quietly, think about it for a while, and then decide to stand up and start cheering. No, when your team scores, you immediately erupt in shouting and clapping. The people in the stands go nuts! This reaction of excitement and joy is automatic. When something good happens, people shout!

Well, I want you to keep that image in mind this week as we read Psalm 136. After every single verse, the author of this Psalm automatically says, "His love endures forever." The phrase is repeated 26 times! The author is so overwhelmed by the love of God that He says it over and over and over again.

This week, we're going to write our own versions of Psalm 136. No, we're not trying to add to Scripture. This is just a way to make this psalm personal. And as you journal this week, you're going to have the opportunity to write out a psalm to God. You see, the psalmist talks about different facets of God's character and work in Psalm 136. We're going to do the same thing. And after every line, we're going to erupt in praise, saying, "His love endures forever!"

So let's get started thinking about who God is and what He has done for us.

Day 1 >

Psalm 136:1-3;
Deuteronomy 10:14-22

Read Psalm 136:1-3. This Psalm starts off by praising God for who He is. The psalmist praises God because He is the God of gods and the Lord of lords. He is the only One who deserves all praise.

Now read Deuteronomy 10:14-22. This passage says the same thing we see in Psalm 136:1-3. God is mighty and awesome and He deserves our praise—not just for what He has done but simply for who He is.

The first verses of Psalm 136 start by saying, "Give thanks to . . ." Then they describe who God is. As we begin writing our own versions of Psalm 136, let's start by simply exalting God for who He is. Write out three or four verses that say, "Give thanks to . . ." filling in the last part of each verse with one of the names of God. For example, you might write, "Give thanks to the King of all kings." Don't forget: After every verse, write the words, "His love endures forever!"

Day 2 >>

Psalm 136:4-9; Psalm 19:1-6

Read Psalm 136:4-9. Notice that the writer praises God for His works in creation. The Psalm talks about the heavens and the earth, the waters and the sun, the moon and the stars. Throughout Scripture, God is praised over and over again for His work in creation. Now read Psalm 19:1-6. These verses tell us that the heavens themselves declare the glory of God. It is almost like all of creation is shouting out that God is great.

The verses we've looked at today in Psalm 136 say, "To Him who . . ." and then they describe the ways God has made the beauty around us. So as you journal today, look at creation, and write at least four ways you see God's greatness around you. For example, you might write, "To Him who made the trees and the flowers . . ." And then don't forget: After every verse, add "His love endures forever!"

Day 3 >>>
Psalm 136:10-22; Psalm 135:8-13

Read Psalm 136:10-22. This is a list of the works God did for His people. In our study of covenant, we have read about many of these. Basically, the psalmist is retelling all of the ways God had been faithful to His people. Read Psalm 135:8-13. Throughout the Old Testament, God's people would praise Him for the acts He had done in their history.

As you continue your version of Psalm 136, spend some time recounting some ways we see God's faithfulness. Think about different Bible stories that show the faithfulness of God. Write out, "To Him who . . .," and then record at least 8 or 10 of the ways God has shown His faithfulness to people in the past. For example, you might write, "To Him who delivered Daniel out of the lion's den," or "To Him who raised Jesus, His Son, from the grave." And then, after every line, write out, "His love endures forever!"

Day 4 >>>>

Psalm 136:23-24;
1 Thessalonians 5:16-18

Read Psalm 136:23-24. For the first time, the author speaks in first person, referring to God as ". . . the One who remembered us . . . and freed us . . ." The psalmist knew God's faithfulness was not just for His people in the past. God's faithfulness was for him, too!

Read 1 Thessalonians 5:16-18. We have reason to be thankful every day. God is faithful to us just like He has always been to His people. The God who was faithful to bring Daniel out of the lion's den is the God who is faithful to you today. What a thought!

As you continue your version of Psalm 136, write about how God has shown His faithfulness to you. Write, "To Him who . . ." and then write at least four sentences that talk about what God has done in your life. You might write, "To Him who saved me from my sins." Make

this psalm personal for your life. After every line, write (you guessed it), "His love endures forever."

Day 5 >>>>>

Psalm 136:25-26; Revelation 5:11-14

Read Psalm 136:25-26. Verse 26 reminds us that God is the God of heaven. In other words, He is Lord over everything. God is not only worthy of our praise; He is worthy of the praise of every creature. Now read Revelation 5:11-14. These verses talk about how God will one day receive the praise of all creation. There will be a day when every person and everything in all of creation will sing praise to God.

As you close out your version of Psalm 136 this week, think about people in your life who may not be following God. Finish Psalm 136 by writing, "Who gives love to . . ." and then end each sentence with the names of people you can share God's love with. You might write, "Who gives love to my best friend, John," or, "Who gives love to every student in my school" or "Who gives love to people living in the Middle East." After every line, close with, "His love endures forever." And then look today for an opportunity to make that love known.

Love for God

memory verse

"Hear, O Israel: The LORD our God, the LORD is one. Love the LORD your God with all your heart and with all your soul and with all your strength." **Deuteronomy 6:4-5**

During a trip to India, I was talking with two Muslims. I asked them if they knew they would go to heaven when they died. They said that they didn't. (Islam is a religion in which you must work in order to earn the approval of Allah.) I told them I knew I was going to heaven. They said that is impossible. So I said to them, "Let me ask you a question. What if I told my wife, 'I love you. I will continue to love you as long as you cook and wash my clothes. But if you stop doing these things, I will stop loving you'?" They agreed this wasn't a very good kind of love.

I looked at the students and said, "Wouldn't it be better if I told my wife I loved her and would always love her, no matter what? Which would be a greater display of love?" They said, "Unconditional love is the greatest display of love." At this I said, "That's the way the God of the Bible loves you. He doesn't love you based on what you do for Him. He loves you based on what Jesus has already done for you."

God's love for us is perfect, but is our love for Him perfect? This week, we're going to be studying two main passages of Scripture: Deuteronomy 6:1-9 and Matthew 22:34-37. They both talk about the greatest commandment in the Bible, the commandment that sums up every other commandment. These are passages we really need to pay attention to! Let's begin to think about what it means to love the God who has poured out unconditional love on us.

covenant: Knowing God—His Relationship with His People

Day 1 >

Deuteronomy 6:1-2; Exodus 19:16-22

Read Deuteronomy 6:1-2. This passage talks about fearing God. But how do you love someone when you're afraid? Well, love and fear go together in our relationship with God. If God did not love us, or we had not accepted His love, we would have a lot of reasons to fear Him. He is all-powerful, He has infinite justice, and He must punish sin.

This is one of the reasons the people of God were so afraid in Exodus 19:16-22. But when we consider that Jesus paid the price for our sins on the cross, we don't need to fear God's wrath anymore. When we approach God, we approach Him in awe and in reverence. But we also approach Him with joy. We know that He has poured out His love on us.

In your journal, ask God to give you a deeper reverence and awe for Him. And as you pray in awe of Him, thank Him for His love, which makes a relationship with Him possible.

Day 2 >>

Deuteronomy 6:3; James 1:22-25

Read Deuteronomy 6:3. The people are told to take two actions: Hear and obey. Hear the Word of the Lord. And then, once you've heard it, obey it. The rest of the verse tells the promises for God's people when they do these two things.

Read James 1:22-25. The New Testament gives the same key to success. Many times in our Christian lives, we forget these keys to success. Sometimes, we don't read our Bible, and so we don't know what we're supposed to obey! Other times, we read God's Word, close our Bibles, and forget what we've read. We will miss out on God's promises if we only hear His Word and we don't obey it!

Write three verses from the Bible that give you commandments to obey. Then write how you are going to obey those commandments today. Pray that God will grant you success as you hear and obey.

Day 3 >>>
Deuteronomy 6:4-5; Matthew 22:34-37

In Matthew 22, a teacher of the law tried to trap Jesus. Guys like this loved to sit around and debate issues from God's Law. Most of the time, they missed the point! So when this guy asked Jesus which was the greatest commandment, Jesus quoted from Deuteronomy 6:5.

Basically, Jesus said, "Love God with all you have. With everything that is in you—your entire heart, your entire mind, your entire soul, all your strength, with everything you have—love God like crazy!" Jesus was saying that this is the one commandment around which every other commandment revolves. We don't follow the commandments because someone makes us or because we have to; we do everything we do because we love God totally.

Journal today about what you believe it means to love God. What does love for God look like in your life? Are there any areas of your life where you are not showing love for God?

Day 4 >> >>

Deuteronomy 6:7-9; Matthew 22:38-39

After telling this guy to love God like crazy, Jesus gave him another commandment: "Love people like crazy!" Jesus told him that the automatic result of love for God is love for people. Now look back at Deuteronomy 6:7-9. God told His people in Deuteronomy to love the people around them enough to pass His Word down to them. The Bible is teaching us something here that is very important. One of the greatest ways we can show love for others is to share God's Word with them.

Journal today about the practical ways you can show love for the people around you. Think specifically about ways you can show love by sharing God's Word.

Think of someone in your life who doesn't know God's love, and pray for an opportunity to share His Word—His love!—with them today.

Day 5 >>>>>

Deuteronomy 6:6; Matthew 22:40

In Matthew 22:40, Jesus told the Pharisee that all of the Law and prophets hang on two commandments: love God and love people. These two commandments are the center of our covenant relationship with God. Everything we do in our relationship with God is summed up in our love for God and our love for people around us.

Look back at Deuteronomy 6:6. God told His people to write these commandments on their hearts. These commandments are to drive everything we do. Let them motivate you every morning when you get out of bed. Let your entire purpose in life be to love God and to love people.

Begin thinking about how you can really love God and truly love people. As you journal today, write two practical ways you can show love to God and two practical ways you can show love to people. Ask God to put these commandments at the center of your heart today.

covenant: Knowing God—His Relationship with His People

Love Obeys

Jesus replied, "If anyone loves me, he will obey my teaching. My Father will love him, and we will come to him and make our home with him." **John 14:23**

I have a tendency to lose things. So I remember well the morning I bought my wife's engagement ring. I needed to go to the mall to get something, but I was afraid some guy would steal my wallet and would find the ring and take it. So even though it was a warm day outside, I got the heaviest coat I had and wrapped the ring in the inside pocket. I put the coat on, put my hand over the pocket with the ring, and walked into the mall.

I remember that day so well because everything about me changed when I had that ring in my possession. The way I walked, talked, acted . . . it all changed when I realized what a valuable possession I had with me.

This week, we're going to see that we have a much more valuable possession than a ring. We have the Holy Spirit living inside of us. When we realize that God has put His Spirit in us, it will change everything about us. His love changes everything about us! And the way we live is a reflection of our love of Him. Let's study John 14:15-24 together this week in order to understand what a valuable possession we have living inside of us.

Day 1 >

John 14:15, 21; 1 John 5:1-5

Many times misguided Christians say things such as, "Well, as long as I love God in my heart, can't I do whatever I want?" This kind of thinking completely misses the point of what it means to love God in your heart. If you truly love God, you will not do whatever you want. Instead, you'll do whatever He wants!

Read John 14:15 and 14:21. Then look at what John says over in 1 John 5:1-5. These verses are pretty clear: anyone who loves Jesus will do whatever He says to do. If someone says they love God, yet they don't obey His Word, that means that don't really love God. True love for God shows itself in obedience.

This is a pretty humbling truth of Scripture. As you journal today, think about areas of your life where you are not being completely obedient to God. How can you express love for God through changing your ways? Ask God to help you love Him with all your heart.

Day 2 >>

John 14:16-20; John 15:26-27

As we read these verses, we need to remember that Jesus was telling these things to His disciples right before He went to the cross. The primary source of comfort

for Jesus' disciples would be the Holy Spirit, whom Jesus would send to them after He rose from the grave.

Read John 14:16 and John 15:26. Both passages refer to the Holy Spirit as the Counselor. This word refers to a person who would provide help in a given situation. Jesus knew His disciples could not live the Christian life on their own. That's one of the reasons He sent the Holy Spirit. But the Holy Spirit was not just for the disciples. The same Comforter lives in us.

As you journal, think about the areas of your Christian life where you need help. How does the Holy Spirit help you in those situations? Pray that God will give you a deeper understanding of the Holy Spirit's purpose in your life this week.

Day 3 >>>
John 14:16-20; John 16:12-15

In addition to comforting them, Jesus told His disciples that the Spirit would guide them. Look over in John 16:12-15. The Spirit will guide us into all truth.

Think about how this relates to loving God. We have already seen that we love God by obeying His commands. But how do we understand what God's commands are? That's where the Holy Spirit comes in. As we study Scripture, the Holy Spirit guides our minds and our hearts so that we understand. And then He leads us to obey the truth that we have learned.

Journal today about why the Holy Spirit is necessary in order for you to understand God's Word. Ask His Spirit to help you understand His truth every time you read or study God's Word and every time you go to a worship service.

Day 4 >>>>
John 14:16-20; Acts 1:8

Read Acts 1:8. These are the words of Jesus right before He ascended into heaven. That means they're pretty important! He told His disciples that when the Holy Spirit would come upon them, they would be witnesses.

A witness in a courtroom has one primary purpose: to give testimony to what He has seen and heard. That's exactly what Jesus was telling these guys to do. In fact, it's the same thing He tells every one of His children: Tell others about what you have seen and heard. Tell your family, your friends, and all people in all nations about the love of God in Christ.

We have the Holy Spirit to comfort us and to guide us. He also wants to empower us to tell others about Christ. You are a witness to His love and His greatness! Record one person you can be a witness to this week. Pray that God will give you power by His Spirit to share testimony with him or her.

John 14:22-24; Romans 8:9-11

We show our love to God by obeying His commands. God has given us His Holy Spirit to comfort us, to guide us, and to empower us to obey His Word and share it with others. Read John 14:22-24. Notice that God makes a home in our hearts as we obey His Word.

When we are enjoying God's love for us and expressing our love to Him, we experience the complete satisfaction of what it means to be in a relationship with God. He is dwelling in us and we are dwelling in Him. This is what covenant is all about!

Hopefully, this week you have thought about your level of obedience to God. As you journal today, write a prayer of love to God that includes your renewed commitment to fully obey Him. Thank God for the opportunity to be in a covenant relationship with Him.

Love One Another

"My command is this: Love each other as I have loved you." **John 15:12**

One of the most dominant characteristics of the New Testament Church was the way its members loved each other. The Church was known in the community around it as a group of sacrificially loving people. When others tried to attack Christianity as a false religion, the leaders of the Church would show that Christianity was real by pointing to the acts of service they were doing in the community. Love was their distinguishing mark!

In a world of TV, Internet, MP3 players, cell phones, and instant messaging, it's easy to lose sight of what it really means to love and serve the people. How can we really care for the people who are hurting around us? In the passage we're going to study together this week, we're going to see Christ's command for His disciples to love each other. Along the way, we're going to think about how we can best demonstrate Christ's love to the people around us—in our families, in our neighborhoods, in our schools, wherever we are.

I'm convinced that if we're going to show that Christianity is true and real in our culture, it's going to happen when we lay down our lives to love other people, just like the early Church was doing. So let's dive in to John 15:9-17 and see what it means to love like Jesus loved.

Day 1 >

John 15:9; John 15:1-8

In order to understand what Jesus was saying in John 15:9, we need to understand what He had just said in John 15:1-8. Jesus referred to Himself as the Vine and to us as branches. Look at verse 5. Based on that verse, what do you think is our main responsibility as Christians?

Your first thought may be that our main responsibility as Christians is to bear fruit. But that's not what this passage is teaching us. According to John 15:5, our main responsibility is to remain in Christ; He will bear fruit through us.

As you journal today, write what you think it means to remain, or abide, in Christ. How important is your time in prayer and Bible study to helping you remain in Christ? Ask God to bear fruit through you today as you pursue Him with all your heart.

Day 2 >>

John 15:10-11; John 3:27-30

As you read John 15:10-11, you'll see two main themes: obedience and joy. We have already seen how we show our love for God by the way we obey His commands. Now look at verse 11. Jesus said that when this happened, His joy would be in us.

Read John 3:27-30. John the Baptist was talking in these verses, and he said that his joy was most complete when he heard Christ's voice. John the Baptist showed the love and glory of Christ to people around him. Don't miss what the Bible is teaching us here! True joy is not found when we indulge in the things of this world; true joy is found when we lay down our lives to show the love and glory of Christ to those around us.

Journal today about two or three practical things you can do to show the love and glory of Christ to people in your life today. Ask God to show you the joy of obeying His command to love each other.

Day 3 >>>
John 15:12-13; 1 John 3:16-18

In John 15:12-13, Jesus basically said, "My command is to love each other." Then He told them to lay down their lives for their friends. That's a pretty bold statement! But Jesus was about to prove His words with actions. Soon He would die on a cross to show the love of God to His people.

Thankfully the chances of us dying on a cross like Jesus are not very high. But the command is the same: to lay down our desires, our wants, and our very lives to serve others. When Jesus washed His disciples' feet in John 13, it was unexpected.

But Jesus laid down His position to serve His disciples.

As you journal today, think about something unexpected you could do to serve someone. Think of a way you could truly lay down your wants and desires to serve someone around you. Then do it, and have confidence that you are loving like Jesus loves.

Day 4 >>>>
John 15:14-15; John 13:34-35

Jesus said some amazing things in John 15:14-15. In those verses He called His disciples His friends. These words weren't just for them but for us! Jesus said we are His friends because we are involved in His mission. He laid down His life; we are to do the same thing.

Read John 13:34-35. Jesus told us that the world will know we are His disciples when we love one another. Jesus is not here physically on the earth today, but just as God's love was shown through Him when He was here, God is now showing His love to the world through us.

God's plan is to show His love through you, just like He was doing with Jesus. Journal today about how you can show the character and life of Jesus through the way you act toward those around you. And thank God for the awesome privilege of being called a friend of Christ!

Day 5 >>>>>

John 15:16-17; John 14:12-14

Prayer is one of the ways we remain in Christ. Read John 15:16-17. Now check out the promise in verse 16: "The Father will give you whatever you ask in my name." Jesus said the Father will give us whatever we ask!

Jesus isn't saying God will give us a new Xbox 360. He's saying that when we are laying down our lives like He calls us to, we can have confidence in prayer. God will answer our prayers so His love will be clearly demonstrated through us. If you really want to see the power of God, start serving and loving like Christ.

As you close this week, write a prayer to God that expresses your desire to love and serve like Jesus commands in this passage. Then pray that God would use you to clearly show His love. And don't forget to be confident that He is going to answer that prayer!

covenant: Knowing God—His Relationship with His People

David and Jonathan

Jonathan said to David, "Go in peace, for we have sworn friendship with each other in the name of the LORD, saying, 'The LORD is witness between you and me, and between your descendants and my descendants forever.'" Then David left, and Jonathan went back to the town. **1 Samuel 20:42**

Years ago, the church where I serve began a homeless ministry in downtown New Orleans. We began by simply sitting down with homeless men and women and getting to know them. Then we started bringing some food with us to give away as we were hanging out. We would bring food, sit around, and get to know the stories of these men and women.

The more I got to know them, the more my desire to be involved in their lives grew. They would tell me and others about their families, the jobs they used to have, and the dreams some of them still had. We brought church to these people, hosting a worship service in the French Quarter every Sunday morning. Many of them would come back to our church, where they would worship with us there. It was amazing to see God's Spirit at work in our church members as they gave themselves to this ministry.

Our homeless ministry was a good picture of covenant. How so? We're going to see this week that our covenant with God has a great effect on our relationships with others. The Bible talks about having covenants with each other that reflect our covenant with God. This week, we're going to see the covenant between two friends, David and Jonathan. We're going to look at four marks of a friendship that has its foundation in God's covenant with us. Hopefully, along the way, we'll learn how to have this kind of friendship in our lives.

Day 1 >

1 Samuel 20:1-3; Proverbs 27:6

This week, we're going to talk about the "covenant friendship" between David and Jonathan. What we mean by a "covenant friendship" is a friendship that has its foundation in God's covenant with us. When two people who are in covenant with God have a friendship, the way they relate to each other is based on their relationship with God. So the first characteristic of a covenant friendship is trust. Read 1 Samuel 20:1-3.

Jonathan trusted David more than he trusted his own father. Throughout this story, we're going to see that these two guys trusted each other completely. It sounds a lot like Proverbs 27:6, which talks about how even the wounds of a close friend can always be trusted.

Think about the people you trust the most. What makes them trustworthy? Then think about the people who trust you. How can you be more trustworthy? Record your thoughts. Ask God today to make you trustworthy and give you friendships with people you can trust.

Day 2 >>

1 Samuel 20:4; Proverbs 27:9

Read 1 Samuel 20:4. Vulnerability is the second characteristic of a covenant

covenant: Knowing God—His Relationship with His People

friendship. Jonathan told David he would be willing to do whatever David asked him to. This is a result of the trust they had. When you trust someone, you are willing to take risks to share your life with that person.

Read Proverbs 27:9. This verse gives a picture of a friend who gives earnest counsel. I have a close friend, a pastor, with whom I share everything. That's what it means to be vulnerable with someone. And when I share those kinds of things with this friend, I know he'll do whatever he can to help me out.

One of the biggest hindrances to this part of a friendship is gossip. Can people trust you when they share things with you? Journal today about how you can create this kind of vulnerability in your relationships with your friends. Pray that God will make you the kind of friend that Jonathan was to David.

Day 3 >>>
1 Samuel 20:5-15; Proverbs 17:17

The third characteristic of a friendship grounded in God's covenant is loyalty. David was sharing important information with Jonathan. Not only was Jonathan trustworthy, but he was also loyal. If you read the rest of the passage, you'll see that. Jonathan was true to his word, exactly as he promised to David.

Read over in Proverbs 17:17. Notice three important words: "at all times." The Bible teaches that a friend loves at all times, not just when things are going well and not just when it's beneficial to love you. A true friend is loyal and committed to you even when no one else is.

Journal today about a time when someone stood by your side in an important time in your life. How did that person's loyalty affect your relationship with him or her? Pray that God will bless you with loyal friends and make you a person whose loyalty is evident in your friendships.

Day 4 >>>>>
1 Samuel 20:16-17; Ecclesiastes 4:10

The final characteristic of a covenant friendship in this passage is sacrifice. Read 1 Samuel 20:16-17. The Bible says Jonathan loved David as he loved himself. It would have been easy for Jonathan to betray David. After all, why was David going to be the next king of Israel? Why not Jonathan? Jonathan easily could have sold out David and taken the throne of Israel himself.

But Jonathan loved David as he did himself. He looked out for David and did whatever he could to help him. This is exactly what Ecclesiastes 4:10 says—a friend helps you when you fall.

Journal today about the effects of selfishness in friendships. Do you look out for your friend's interest more than your own? Pray that God will make you that kind of person and give you friendships that are characterized by selflessness and sacrifice.

Day 5 >> >> >>

1 Samuel 20:42; Proverbs 18:24

Think about the four characteristics of covenant friendships: trust, vulnerability, loyalty, and sacrifice. Now think about the covenant God has made with us. These characteristics describe God's relationship with us. He is worthy of our trust; we can be vulnerable in expressing our cares to Him; He is loyal at all times; and He gave His Son as a sacrifice for our salvation.

Our friendships must be founded in our relationship with God. God has demonstrated these characteristics through His covenant. In light of His relationship with us, He calls us to reflect His covenant in our friendships with one another.

As we close out the week, journal about how many true covenant friendships you have. You may have many or none. Either way, pray that God would give you this kind of friendship. Pray for a deeper understanding of God's covenant so you can know how best to build friendships with those around you.

David and Mephibosheth

"Don't be afraid," David said to him, "for I will surely show you kindness for the sake of your father Jonathan. I will restore to you all the land that belonged to your grandfather Saul, and you will always eat at my table."

2 Samuel 9:7

Last week, I told you about the homeless ministry run by our church in New Orleans. During the early days of this ministry, a friend and I invited two men who were homeless to church. Their names were Eric and Kenneth. After church, we took them to a great seafood restaurant. We walked in, sat down, and began to look at the menus. Immediately, Eric leaned across the table and looked at me and said, "Are you sure you can afford this?"

It wasn't that expensive, but it was nicer than where he was used to eating. We told them to get whatever they wanted. Both chose the seafood platter— basically a mound of shrimp, catfish, and oysters. We ordered, and the waitress brought out our food. Imagine the looks on these guys' faces who were used to eating out of dumpsters. Their eyes were huge! Quickly they began to dig in. They went back to the French Quarter that day with bags of leftovers!

We will find the same kind of excitement in this week's passage. We're going to see a guy with a pretty wild name, Mephibosheth, come to the table of King David. As we study this passage, we'll see the covenant friendship between David and Jonathan that began in last week's study come full circle. We'll also see a picture of the grace of God, who one day is going to allow you and me to dine at the King's table for all of eternity.

covenant: Knowing God—His Relationship with His People

2 Samuel 9:1; 1 Samuel 20:8-15

As we begin our journey through 2 Samuel 9, we need to start by going back to part of the passage we read last week. Read 1 Samuel 20:8-15. Remember the covenant David and Jonathan had made together? David said he would never cut off his kindness from Jonathan or his family.

In the years that followed, both Saul and Jonathan, David's best friend, died. David's heart was deeply grieved. But at the same time, it was David's time to ascend to the throne. When we come to 2 Samuel 9:1, we see an incredible picture of David's loyalty to Jonathan. Amid all that David had the responsibility to do as king, he still took the time to keep his promise to Jonathan.

Journal today about any promises you have made in the friendships you have. Are you keeping those promises? Pray today that God would use you to reflect His loyalty in your relationships with others.

2 Samuel 9:2-3; Ephesians 4:29-32

The word "kindness" is repeated three times in this passage, in verses 1, 3, and 7. David was looking to find out if anyone from Jonathan's family whom he could show God's kindness to was still alive.

David's search led him to Mephibosheth. Imagine having to learn to spell that name as a kid! We're going to learn more about Mephibosheth tomorrow, but for now, we are seeing that David was committed to showing kindness to anyone who was from Jonathan's family. He knew the kindness of God was reflected in the covenant he had with Jonathan.

Read Ephesians 4:29-32, paying close attention to the last verse. How can you live out Ephesians 4:32 today? Journal about some practical things you can do, and pray that God would use you to display His kindness in unexpected ways.

Day 3 >>>

2 Samuel 9:4-10; 2 Samuel 4:4

David found Mephibosheth, one of Jonathan's sons who was still alive. Go back and read 2 Samuel 4:4. Because of his defect, Mephibosheth was most likely rejected by people. But look at how David treated him. He welcomed him into his palace and invited him to dinner!

See how Mephibosheth responded in verse 8. He called himself a "dead dog." Mephibosheth was afraid of what David might do to him, but David showered him with God's kindness. Here is a picture we see throughout Scripture: God's people are called to shower His kindness on the people in society who are rejected by everyone else.

Journal today about how you can put this into practice in your life. What can you do to reach out to those teenagers who no one else reaches out to? How can you befriend them in order that they might see the kindness of God in you?

Day 4 >>>>
2 Samuel 9:11;
2 Samuel 19:24-30

So David invited Mephibosheth to eat at his table, but not just for one meal. David invited this guy to be there for every meal. And so Mephibosheth packed his bags and moved out of Lo Debar and into Jerusalem. His life was changed forever!

Read 2 Samuel 19:24-30. David and Mephibosheth still had a close relationship with each other. You see, David's commitment to keeping his covenant with Jonathan didn't stop with his invitation for Jonathan's son to have a meal with him. Throughout the rest of Mephibosheth's life, David kept his covenant with Jonathan's family.

Throughout our lives, we have friendships that come and go. But along the way, we encounter a small number of people whom we will keep in touch with for the rest of our lives. Journal today about what characteristics mark this kind of friendship. How does our relationship with God help these friendships continue?

Day 5 >>>>>
2 Samuel 9:12-13; Revelation 21:6-7

As we come to the end of 2 Samuel 9, we see a summary of the story. The Bible says Mephibosheth was always eating at King David's table. And once again, we are reminded that this crippled man had the privilege of being with the king for the remainder of his life.

This story is definitely a picture of David's covenant friendship with Jonathan. But it's deeper than that. It's an illustration of God's love for us. Look over in Revelation 21:6-7. The Bible promises that everyone who trusts in Christ will one day drink freely from a spring of living water. And just like Mephibosheth, our eternity will be sealed in His presence.

Journal today about the covenant love God has shown you. Then think about how you can display that same covenant love with those around you today. As you pray, thank God for His gracious invitation to dine at His table for all of eternity!

Binding Love

Love is patient, love is kind. It does not envy, it does not boast, it is not proud.

1 Corinthians 13:4

I recently heard a man who grew up in India speaking at a conference. He was talking about how many of the marriages in India have traditionally been arranged marriages. In other words, your mom and dad would find a spouse for you. There's no dating process. You would be arranged to marry a particular person of their choosing.

This speaker told a story about his brother's arranged marriage. The family made extremely involved preparations for the wedding. The speaker remembers sitting his brother down one day and saying to him, "What if you walk into the room, look at this woman, and realize you can't marry her?" His brother said to him, "You think love is based on emotion and feeling. I believe love is based on an act of your will. No matter what, I am going to choose to marry the woman that is arranged for me to marry." And that's exactly what the brother did. More than 20 years later, that brother was still married to his wife.

Love is a choice. It goes a lot deeper than an emotion or a feeling. It's a decision of the will. This week, we're going to study a famous passages about love: 1 Corinthians 13. We're going to discover the love we are called to show other people goes a lot deeper than just emotions or feelings. We have to choose to show the perfect love of Christ to others. Let's dive in and see what perfect love is all about.

Day 1 >

1 Corinthians 13:1-13; John 17:26

Read through the entire chapter of 1 Corinthians 13, and circle the amount of times you see the word "love." The Bible uses many different words to describe love. The word for love in 1 Corinthians 13 is *agape*, which literally means complete or perfect love.

Read John 17:26. Here we see the same word for love, agape, mentioned by Jesus. He is talking about the love He has for God the Father and the love the Father has for Him. That's the most perfect love you can imagine. What we're going to see this week is that God has not only shown you and me this kind of love, but He also wants to use us to show this love to the world.

Journal today about what makes God's love for you perfect. How would you describe God's love for you? As you pray today, thank God for His unconditional, perfect love for His children.

Day 2 >>

1 Corinthians 13:1-3; Philippians 2:1-5

To understand why this chapter is so important, we need to understand the context. Paul was writing to the church at Corinth, which had become divided. A lot of conflict existed in the church. One of

covenant: Knowing God—His Relationship with His People

the biggest issues was the issue of spiritual gifts. People were bragging about which gifts the Holy Spirit had given them.

This is the main theme in 1 Corinthians 12-14. Right in the middle, Paul reminded the Christians that it doesn't matter if you have spiritual gifts if you don't have love. Read 1 Corinthians 13:1-3. Then read Philippians 2:1-5. In those verses, he was encouraging the church to be unified by focusing on the love of Christ.

God's love brings unity in the Church, not division. How can you make sure God's love stays at the center of your youth group so that you stay unified? Journal and pray today about what you can do to keep God's love central among the students at your church.

Day 3 >>>
1 Corinthians 13:4-7; John 15:12-14

As we read 1 Corinthians 13:4-7, we see love described in positive ways and negative ways. For example, positively, this passage says love is patient, kind, rejoices with the truth, always protects, trusts, hopes, and perseveres. But then the passage also speaks negatively, describing what love doesn't do. Love does not envy, boast, get conceited or easily angered, or keep any record of wrongs.

This is what love looks like in action. It's exactly what Jesus encouraged His disciples to do back in John 15:12-14: Put your love into action! We love not only by the things we do but also by the things we don't do.

Journal today about these two sides of love. Make a list of actions you can take to show love today, and then make a list of actions you can avoid in order to show love. Ask God to show His love in action through your life today.

Day 4 >>>>
1 Corinthians 13:8-10; Psalm 89:24-29

After Paul described love, he described love's main advantage. Paul said that love is permanent; it never fails. Gifts pass way. The things of this world pass away. But love is different. Love never passes away.

Read Psalm 89:24-29, an incredible promise for David and God's people. God will maintain His love to us forever. In this world, we sometimes worry about people loving us for a while, and then leaving us. This might be a mom, dad, boyfriend, girlfriend, or another close friend. Isn't it good to know that there is a relationship you can always count on? God's love to you will never fail!

Record your thoughts about the security of knowing God's love will never fail.

Then think about someone in your life who does not know the love of God. How can you share His love today so that they, too, might know that we can have a relationship with God that will never fail.

Day 5 >>>>>
1 Corinthians 13:13; 1 John 4:16-21

Paul wrote that many things will fail. But faith, hope, and love will remain forever. He made it clear that love is supreme over all of these things, ". . . the greatest of these is love." Read 1 John 4:16-21. In that passage, we see the love of God described pretty clearly.

Continue to read in 1 John 4. See how John wrote about how we love others because Christ loved us first? Our love for God and our love for each other is grounded in God's love for us. His covenant love is the foundation for the love we show, not only to Him but also to everyone around us.

Journal today about how you can show love to God in light of His love for you. Then write some ways you can love, people around you. Praise God for His great love and commit yourself to loving Him and others with the same kind of love.

The New Covenant

In 2005, C.S. Lewis' *The Lion, the Witch, and the Wardrobe* came alive on movie screens across the country. Near the end of the movie, Aslan, the lion who in many ways represents Christ, made a deal with the evil White Witch. Aslan offered to give his life in order to save the life of Edmund, a boy in the story who had betrayed his brother and sisters. Lucy and Susan, Edmond's sisters, watched in horror as Aslan was brutally murdered. After everyone left, Lucy and Susan, sobbing, made their way back to the place where Aslan lay. But as the day began to break, they heard a strange sound and looked behind them only to find Aslan gone. He had risen from the dead and was standing right behind them!

C.S. Lewis' novel has its foundation in the death and resurrection of Christ. When Christ, who was without sin, died for our sins on the cross, He conquered death and earned eternal life for you and me. This is what covenant is all about. Throughout our study of covenant, we've seen the important role blood played in sacrifices. It was Jesus' blood that would be central in the new supreme covenant of the New Testament.

This week, we're going to join in Jesus' last meal with His disciples before He went to the cross. What did He say to them that was so important, and what does it have to do with our relationship to God? Why was innocent blood necessary for the new covenant? Let's dive in and see.

covenant: Knowing God—His Relationship with His People

Luke 22:15-18;
1 Corinthians 11:23-26

Read Luke 22:15-18. The Lord's Supper was not just about what Jesus was going to do on the cross. In the middle of the Lord's Supper, Jesus implied that He would eat and drink with them again in the future . . . after He died! This week, we're going to focus on Jesus' death and how it provides forgiveness for our sins.

Now read 1 Corinthians 11:23-26. This idea was huge for the first-century Christians. They would celebrate and participate in the Lord's Supper, not just as a reminder of what Jesus did on the cross but as a reminder that one day they would eat and drink with Him again. The Lord's Supper contains Jesus' promise that He is coming back!

Is Jesus' return something you think about often? What kind of difference does it make when we are anticipating the second coming of Jesus?

Luke 22:19; Isaiah 53:1-12

In Luke 22:19, Jesus told His disciples He was about to give His body as a sacrifice. Now read Isaiah 53:1-12. This is aprophecy of God's salvation through the sacrifice of Jesus.

God's strategy in the Bible was to show His love to the world through Jesus' suffering. Does that mean God shows His love to the world through us as we suffer? We all go through difficult times. Some of us experience more than others. But it is in those times that we have the greatest opportunity to show God's love and grace. When we trust in God when things aren't going well, people will see that God takes care of us.

Journal today about a time when you experienced difficulty or suffering. How did you show God's love to those around you during that time? Pray for God to strengthen you so you trust Him no matter what happens in the circumstances around you.

Day 3 >>>
Luke 22:19; 1 Peter 1:17-21

Read Luke 22:19. When we celebrate the Lord's Supper, our primary focus should be on remembering Him. We have a tendency to forget this. As we take the Lord's Supper, we may start thinking about the benefits of forgiveness, that we have eternal life in heaven, and other advantages of salvation. All of these things are wonderful to think about. But remember, Jesus said first and foremost to simply remember Him. Remember who He was, what He did, and who He is in your life today.

covenant: Knowing God—His Relationship with His People

Read 1 Peter 1:17-21. These verses remind us of the seriousness of the blood of Christ. He is our Savior. Without Him, we would be separated from God's love forever.

Today write a prayer to Jesus simply remembering who He was, what He did, and who He is in your life. Spend time today adoring Him as your Savior and the Master of your life.

Day 4 >>>>
Luke 22:20; Exodus 24:1-8

Read Luke 22:20. Jesus told His disciples that the cup represented the blood of the new covenant. These guys knew what He was talking about. A covenant had to be confirmed with a blood sacrifice.

Read Exodus 24:1-8. Moses sprinkled blood on the people to confirm God's covenant with them. You may wonder: "Couldn't Jesus have brought salvation without having to die for us?" The answer is no. We have all sinned against God. The only way to enter into a new covenant with Him is through the blood of One who had no sin. Through His death on the cross, the blood of Jesus covers our sins, bringing us into covenant with God. It's important for us to confess our sin to God. When we do, we are reminded that we are forgiven by the blood of Christ!

Spend some time today in confession. Then, write a praise to Jesus for His blood which covers your sins.

Day 5 >>>>>

Luke 22:20; Jeremiah 31:31-34

Read Jeremiah 31:31-34. Take a moment to list some of the differences mentioned between the old covenant (the covenant in the Old Testament) and new covenant (the covenant through Jesus' blood).

Look closely at Jeremiah 31:34. In the new covenant, God forgives our wickedness and remembers our sins no more. His forgiveness is guaranteed forever! This brings incredible comfort and security to our lives. We don't have to worry about death because, just as Aslan did in C.S. Lewis' writings, Jesus has completely destroyed death so we can experience eternal life. What a promise!

Journal today about the importance of having an everlasting covenant with God. How does Jesus' promise of eternal forgiveness and eternal life bring you comfort and strength? Thank God for the security of eternal life, and pray that He will use you today to lead others to experience that same security.

covenant: Knowing God—His Relationship with His People

Reconciled to God

memory verse

But God demonstrates his own love for us in this: While we were still sinners, Christ died for us.

Romans 5:8

In 2005, the people of Alaska wanted to build a bridge that would go from a small town called Ketchikan, Alaska, to a smaller island called Gravina Island. The population of the island was 50 people. But the bridge, designed to be as long as the Golden Gate Bridge and taller than the Brooklyn Bridge, was to cost $315 million.

The people wanted the bridge because there was no way for the 50 inhabitants of Gravina Island to drive all the way home. They had to take a seven-minute ferry ride in order to get from the town out to the island. When the rest of the country heard the bridge would cost $315 million, they got mad. The project was labeled, "The Bridge to Nowhere."

As we read from Romans 5, we're going to see the word "reconcile." This word is huge for our understanding of covenant. Reconciling is like building a bridge between two things. If two people were separated in their relationship, they would have to reconcile (or build a bridge) in order to come together. Our sin separated us from God, but God reconciled us to Himself. How? He built a bridge; that's what the cross is all about. This bridge is not "The Bridge to Nowhere," and it didn't cost $315 million. This bridge leads to eternal life, and it cost Jesus His life. Let's see how God has brought reconciliation to you and me.

Day 1 >

Romans 5:6; Galatians 4:1-7

In Romans 5:6, Paul says that Christ died for us "at just the right time." The bridge was built when we needed it most. Read Galatians 4:1-7. Paul uses a similar phrase in verse 4, where he says that God sent Jesus "when the time had fully come." What do you think this means?

Paul is saying that, at the exact time set by God the Father, Christ came to the earth. Before that time, the people had the Law of God. We've learned through our study of covenant that the Law couldn't save the people. Romans 5:6 says that they were "powerless"—completely unable to save themselves. That's when God, in His grace, made a bridge by sending Christ to die for all humanity.

Journal today about how you are powerless without Christ. Why is He necessary in your life? What would life be like without Him? Pray that God will help you to understand the importance of Jesus' death on the cross.

Day 2 >>

Romans 5:7-8; Psalm 14:1-3

Read Romans 5:7-8. Notice the contrast: On one side, we see Jesus. We know that Jesus is completely good. He never sinned. He is completely loving and perfectly holy. On

covenant: Knowing God—His Relationship with His People

the other side, we see ourselves. We are full of sin. Our lives are corrupt. Often, our greatest love is not for others but for ourselves. Read Psalm 14:1-3. This is a description of us.

Paul set up this contrast. Then he said something amazing: Christ, who is completely good and loving, died for us, who are just the opposite. Jesus died for us, even though we could never deserve or justify such an incredible gift.

Journal today about the value we have in Christ. How does Jesus' death make us valuable? How does His death change the way we look at ourselves? Thank God for showing His grace to us when we didn't deserve it.

Day 3 >>>
Romans 5:6-11; 2 Corinthians 5:16-21

Read Romans 5:6-11, and circle every time you see the words "died for." This is a phrase we see throughout Scripture and even use pretty often, but what does it really mean?

Read 2 Corinthians 5:16-21. Paul is talking again about reconciliation. These verses basically tell us Jesus died on our behalf, instead of us, in our place. We deserve death and the judgment of God. But Jesus stepped in and took the judgment in our place. He died so we wouldn't have to experience eternal death. This is truly the best news in the world. Yet we're surrounded by people every day who still haven't received the love of Christ.

Journal today about why you think some people have not received His love. Then pray that God will give you an opportunity to tell others that Jesus died for them!

Day 4 >>>>
Romans 5:9-10; Philippians 2:12-13

Read Romans 5:9-10. Paul talks about salvation as being something in the past and the future. Huh? What exactly does that mean? Well, let's take a closer look.

Our salvation is not just something that happened in the past. And it's not just something that's going to happen in the future. It's both! Read Philippians 2:12-13. We're still supposed to be working out our salvation each day. Now, don't get confused; when we profess our belief in Christ, we are saved. But that's just the beginning. As we mature in our faith, we realize all the blessings of our salvation. One day, when we die, we'll experience the ultimate joy of our salvation: eternal life in heaven with God!

Journal today about what it means for you to be saved. What does that mean for

you in the past? What about the present? And what does your salvation mean for your future?

Day 5 >>>>>

Romans 5:11; Romans 5:1-5

Read Romans 5:1-5 and Romans 5:11. Circle every time you see the word rejoice. This passage is not just telling us what it means to be saved. It is telling us to rejoice in our salvation!

We have a lot of reasons to rejoice. Romans 5:1-5 says we can rejoice when we face suffering. How can that be? Because we have hope. We know that one day we will be in heaven with God, saved from His wrath, and enjoying His presence. The only way this is possible is through the bridge Jesus made for us.

As you close out the week, write a prayer of rejoicing to God. Simply thank Him and praise Him for the salvation He has given to you, even though you didn't deserve it. Worship Him for the hope that allows you to rejoice even in the midst of difficult times that you face.

Reconciled to One Another

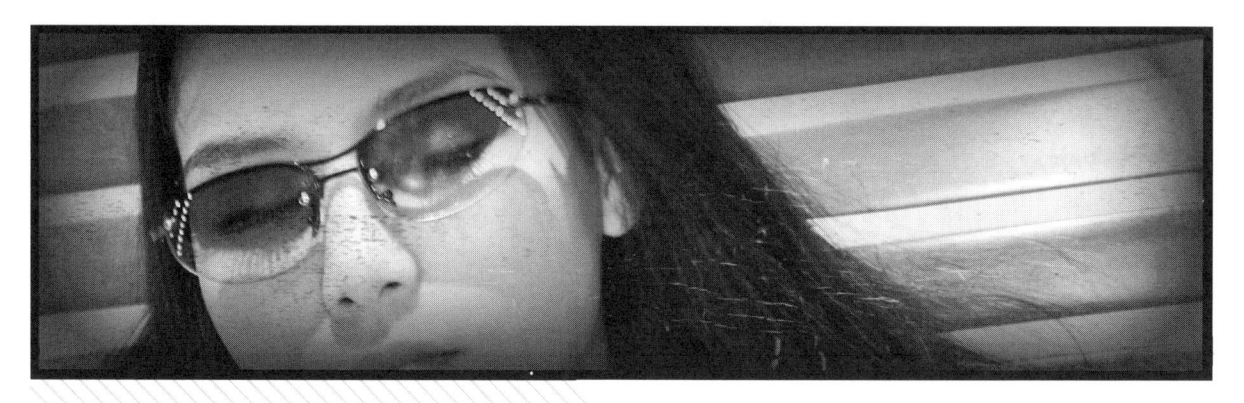

Remember that at that time you were separate from Christ, excluded from citizenship in Israel and foreigners to the covenants of the promise, without hope and without God in the world. But now in Christ Jesus you who once were far away have been brought near through the blood of Christ. **Ephesians 2:12-13**

Going to another country is an interesting experience. You have to make adjustments when you are a foreigner, or an alien, in another country. You have to adjust to the food. (I can still remember watching my wife eat duck feet and pig ear in one Asian country!) You have to adjust to wearing different clothes. (Women in India wear dresses covering themselves from head to ankles while women in the hot regions of Africa have never seen a long dress.) You have to adjust to the language. (I always wonder if people are talking about me.) Fitting in is a real challenge.

This was the challenge the Gentile Christians were facing when Paul wrote the book of Ephesians. Remember, God originally established His covenant with the people of Israel—the Jewish people. But many non-Jewish people (or Gentiles) were coming to faith in Christ. Some of the Jewish people were wondering if it was okay for a Gentile to be in the family of God. After all, they were aliens, right?

That's why we have this passage in Ephesians 2:11-22. In Christ, all people come together, whether they are Jews or Gentiles. This week, we're going to look at the unity that Christ brings to the Church, and we're going to think about how that unity may or may not be reflected in our churches and our youth groups. So let's study this passage that tells us we aren't aliens anymore in the family of God.

Ephesians 2:11; Galatians 5:2-6

In Ephesians 2:11, Paul starts by talking about circumcision. Now, we remember from all that we have studied how important circumcision was. It was the symbol of the covenant God had made with His people. But there was a problem. The Gentiles weren't circumcised. Did that mean they weren't able to be in covenant with God?

Read Galatians 5:2-6. In this passage, Paul said that circumcision does not matter as much as faith in Christ that expresses itself through love. A Gentile Christian was as much a Christian as a Jewish Christian because having Christ in your heart is what makes you a Christian.

Do you think a lot of people today still think being a Christian is about what we do on the outside? For example, do you think people still think that just going to church will make them a Christian? Journal today about what it truly means to be a Christian.

Ephesians 2:12-13; Galatians 4:8

Christ makes the difference. That's the message of Ephesians 2:12-13. Look at the ways Paul described the Gentiles. He said they were separate, excluded from citizenship in Israel, foreigners to the covenant, without hope, and without

God. That's not a good thing. Now read the first words of verse 13: "But now . . ." Paul goes on to talk about the difference Christ had made in their lives.

The Gentiles used to be separated from God; now they were reconciled to God. They used to be excluded from citizenship; now they were in the family of God. They used to be foreigners to the covenant; now they were enjoying the covenant. And all of this happened because of Christ!

As you journal today, write some sentences that describe what you used to be before you put your faith in Christ and then what you are now as a result of your faith in Christ. Spend time thanking God for the difference He has made in your life through Christ.

Day 3 >>>
Ephesians 2:14-16; Colossians 3:15-17

We know God builds the bridge between Himself and us through Christ on the cross. These verses talk about another bridge God builds through Christ on the cross, the bridge between you and me. In Paul's day, a lot of division existed between the Jews and the Gentiles. In Christ, they were being brought together.

Read Ephesians 2:14-16 and Colossians 3:15-17. In these passages, God talks about the peace that happens when His Church comes together as "one body." When we believe in what Christ did on the cross, God not only unites us with Himself, but He also unites us with each other.

Think about your church and your youth group today. Do you see this kind of unity? Journal today about what you can do to create more unity among the Christians around you. Ask God to help bring unity and reconciliation among Christians in your church.

Day 4
Ephesians 2:17-18; Matthew 28:16-20

Read Ephesians 2:17-18. Christ had preached peace to those who were "far away" and those who were "near." For the Jewish people, the area around Jerusalem would be considered near and other places farther away. But the message of the Gospel was not just for Jerusalem; it was for all people everywhere!

Read Matthew 28:16-20. Notice that Jesus commanded His disciples to make this good news known in all nations. We need to realize that the gospel is not just for those who are close to the Church. It is for those who are far away from the Church. It is for all people in all nations.

How are you involved in taking the gospel to people who are far away? Journal today about those in your neighborhood or school who seem far from the gospel. Pray for a chance to share with them. Then pray that God will give you the opportunity to make His gospel known in places far away, even if that means leaving the U.S.

Day 5 >>>>>

Ephesians 2:19-22; 1 Corinthians 3:10-15

At the end of Ephesians 2:19-22, Paul used imagery to help describe Christ's role in bringing the Church together. After Paul told the Gentiles they were no longer foreigners in the Church, he stated Christ is the Chief Cornerstone of the Church. The cornerstone of a building is what holds the entire structure together. That's exactly what Christ does in the Church.

Paul talked about a similar thing in 1 Corinthians 3:10-15, referring to Christ as the foundation. As we focus our lives on Christ and pursue Him with all of our hearts, then the automatic result is that we will come together as a Church.

Journal today about the kinds of things that sometimes bring disunity in your church or in your youth group. How does focusing on Christ help bring the church together? Pray that God will bring unity in your church and in your youth group through Christ as the Chief Cornerstone.

The First Covenant's Shortfall

memory verse

How much more, then, will the blood of Christ, who through the eternal Spirit offered himself unblemished to God, cleanse our consciences from acts that lead to death, so that we may serve the living God! **Hebrews 9:14**

I remember visiting Washington, D.C., with my wife. We were so excited. Every day, we would get up early and spend all day sightseeing: the Washington Monument, the Lincoln Memorial, the Capitol, the Vietnam and D-Day Memorials, and the different museums. But the one place I really wanted to go was the White House. We went to the White House and asked the Secret Service agents if taking a tour would be possible. They told me I should have applied three months before. Needless to say, I was pretty disappointed.

As we read Hebrews 9:1-10 this week, we're going to learn about a house, or tent, of worship called the Tabernacle. And if you think the White House is a hard place to get into, you haven't seen anything until you read about the Tabernacle. Once a year, only one person—the high priest—was allowed to go into the Most Holy Place in the Tabernacle. And even when he did go inside, he was afraid for his life. But that's where he had to go in order to offer the sacrifices for the people of God.

This week, we're going to look at some more differences between the old covenant and the new covenant and how they relate to our lives. We're going to think specifically about our worship. How can we come before God to worship Him? Let's see what credentials you need to get into His presence.

Day 1 >

Hebrews 9:1-10;
1 Corinthians 6:18-20

This week, we're going to read through Hebrews 9:1-10 every day. We'll also look at other Scripture that will help us understand what this passage means. As you read Hebrews 9:1-10 today, try to get a picture of the way things worked in the Tabernacle.

This passage refers to three areas of the Tabernacle: the outer room, an inner room called the Holy Place, and then a room even farther inside called the Most Holy Place. A curtain separated each of these places. The Tabernacle was the "earthly" dwelling for God. The Tabernacle was the place where God's people would go to encounter His presence in worship.

Read 1 Corinthians 6:18-20. Here we learn that we take the presence of God with us wherever we go. Journal today about what it means to always be in the presence of God. How does this affect the way you live? Does this mean that worship should happen all the time?

Day 2 >>

Hebrews 9:1-10;
Leviticus 16:18-22

Once a year, the priest would go into the Most Holy Place to sprinkle blood on the altar. You can read about it in Leviticus

16:18-22. This is how God had arranged for the atonement, or payment, of sins.

During the year, the people would break the laws of the covenant through their disobedience to God. So in order to continue in covenant with God, the people had to send the high priest in once a year to sprinkle the blood on the altar.

In the Old Testament, a blood sacrifice was necessary to pay for the people's sins. During this ceremony, they took confession of their sins very seriously. Unfortunately, today we sometimes take confession of sins lightly. As you journal today, set aside some serious time for prayer and confession. Are there areas of your life where you have been disobedient to Him? Record your thoughts.

Day 3 >>>

Hebrews 9:1-10; Exodus 28:31-35

The rules for worship and entering the presence of God made for an intense experience. Read Exodus 28:31-35. The high priest would attach bells to his robe so he could be heard moving around the Holy Place or the Most Holy Place. If he were struck down in the presence of God, the bells would stop sounding, and the people outside would know he had died.

Talk about intense! The Israelites were not handling the presence of God lightly. They knew it was a very serious thing to be in the presence of God, praying and making offerings to Him.

Do you think we sometimes become too casual with the presence of God? Journal today about what it means to have reverence in God's presence. How does this affect the way you conduct yourself in a church or youth group worship service? How does this affect your everyday life?

Day 4 >>>>
Hebrews 9:1-10;
Hebrews 4:14-16

One of the major differences between the old covenant and the new covenant deals with our access to God. Under the old covenant, few people had the privilege of entering the presence of God. A priest or the high priest would enter into His presence as a representative of all the people of God.

Is a priest still necessary for us to enter the presence of God today? Actually, yes … but maybe not in the way you are thinking. We already have a priest who represents us before God. His name is Jesus. Read Hebrews 4:14-16. Jesus is our great High priest. And because He's our priest, we have unlimited access to God.

Record your thoughts on what it means to have unlimited access to God. Do you take

covenant: Knowing God—His Relationship with His People

advantage of the unlimited access we have to God? Thank Jesus for being our great High Priest who allows us to boldly come before God at all times.

Day 5

Hebrews 9:1-10; Hebrews 7:18-25

Hebrews 9:1-10 shows that, while the old covenant provided for the forgiveness of sins, it couldn't "clear the conscience" of the people. They knew they still had sin. They knew that on their own, they would never be able to have complete victory over sin, no matter how many sacrifices they offered.

That's why Jesus was necessary to complete the covenant. Read Hebrews 7:18-25. In verses 24-25, you see that Jesus is a permanent priest who is able to save us completely. That means He not only saves us from the punishment for our sins, but He also saves us from the power of sin altogether. Because of His sacrifice, we are able to have victory over sin.

Journal today about any sins you have been struggling with recently. Remember that Jesus not only saves you from the punishment of those sins but also from their power in your life. As you confess your sins, ask Him to empower you to have victory over them today.

The New Covenant's Superiority

memory verse

Just as man is destined to die once, and after that to face judgment, so Christ was sacrificed once to take away the sins of many people; and he will appear a second time, not to bear sin, but to bring salvation to those who are waiting for him.
Hebrews 9:27-28

My church in New Orleans began a ministry to those who lived downtown. We started by taking a survey to get an idea of these people's spiritual beliefs. Their responses to our questions were very interesting! One question we asked was, "What happens after you die?" Here are some responses: "You spend an eternity in the place of your choice." "It depends on how you live your life." "Reincarnation." "You're up for grabs; you better have faith then."

Then we asked, "How certain are you that you will spend eternity in heaven when you die?" "I don't believe in heaven, but if there is a heaven, I'm 100 percent sure I would go there." "I am certain because I don't do enough bad things to go to hell." "Very certain . . . compared to Saddam Hussein, I'm an OK guy!" "I'm certain because I have lived my life helping others."

Most people felt they had to do something to get to heaven. What most of them didn't realize is that, with His sacrifice on the cross, Jesus has already done everything to make a way into heaven.

Let's take a closer look into what it means to have a guaranteed future. Let's look at Hebrews 9 and see that our future in heaven is based solely on the sacrifice of Christ for us.

covenant: Knowing God—His Relationship with His People

Hebrews 9:11; Hebrews 10:1

Read Hebrews 9:11 and Hebrews 10:1. In order for us to be perfectly united in a covenant relationship with God, it is necessary that someone take our sins away. That's exactly what this passage is all about.

The more we know about Jesus as we study God's Word, the more we realize all of the "good things" that are ours in Christ. As we grow in our relationship with God, we experience His goodness each day. One day, we are going to be united with Christ in heaven. Then we will fully realize all the "good things" He provides for us.

Journal today about the "good things" we can experience as a result of what Christ did for us on the cross. List the benefits of knowing God through Christ, and along the way, praise Him for all the "good things" He has given us.

Hebrews 9:12; Matthew 7:21-23

Read Hebrews 9:12. As we have studied the sacrificial system, did you ask, "Why did God tell His people to do this?" Good question. But this Old Testament system points to Jesus. The old covenant was based on the sacrifices you could bring to pay for your sins. The new covenant is based on the sacrifice Christ has already paid for your sins.

Read Matthew 7:21-23. A lot of religious people are going to be surprised when they miss out on heaven because they relied on their good works to get them there. No matter how good a religious life we lead, nothing we can do will pay the price for our sins.

Many people today think that religion and good works will get them to heaven. But Christ has already paid the price. Journal today about someone you can share this good news with. Then write down a prayer that God would give you an opportunity to share Christ with that person.

Day 3 >>>

Hebrews 9:12; Ruth 4:13-15

Read Hebrews 9:12. What does the word "redemption" mean? Look back at Ruth 4:13-15. It's the story of a man, Boaz, who redeemed a woman named Ruth. In order for Ruth to become a part of his family, Boaz had to pay a price in order to free, or release, her from her current state.

Think about how this relates to Jesus. We were separated from God, unable to be a part of His family because of our sin. But Jesus has redeemed us. He has paid the price so we could be set free from our sin and become children of God. What a great word . . . redemption!

As you journal today, write out a brief story describing how you were redeemed. What happened when Christ came into your life? What did He free you from, and what did you receive because of the price He paid? Thank Jesus today for obtaining redemption for you!

Day 4 >>>>

Hebrews 9:13-14; Numbers 19:1-10

Read Hebrews 9:13-14. This passage shows how people who were unclean would have the blood of goats and bulls and the ashes of a heifer sprinkled on them to make them clean. That's exactly what the Old Testament talks about in Numbers 19:1-10.

Hebrews 9:13-14 is careful to show us that Jesus was an unblemished sacrifice. He had to be perfectly clean, without sin, in order to pay the price for our sins. And this is an encouraging truth when we think about our struggles with sin. Jesus has conquered every temptation and has said "no" to every struggle with sin. When we struggle with sin, He alone can give us the power to stay clean and holy by resisting temptation.

Journal today about a sin you are struggling with. How can Jesus make you clean from that sin? How can He give you power to resist that sin? Ask Him to cleanse you and make you holy today.

Day 5 >>>>>>

Hebrews 9:15, 27-28; Ephesians 1:13-14

Hebrews 9:27 is a pretty intense verse. Every single one of us is destined to die and face judgment. But the good news comes in the next verse: Christ has sacrificed His life so we don't have to worry about that day. He has promised to come back, and He has promised eternal salvation to everyone who trusts in Him.

What an amazing confidence! You can know for sure that because of faith in Christ's sacrifice for you, you are guaranteed eternal life in heaven. It's exactly what we've read about before in Ephesians 1:13-14. You don't have to worry about what happens when you die because your inheritance is guaranteed!

How does this truth affect the way you live today? And who can you share this incredible truth with? Thank God today for the sacrifice of Christ that makes it possible for us to never fear death.

covenant: Knowing God—His Relationship with His People

Remembering the New Covenant

memory verse

A man ought to examine himself before he eats of the bread and drinks of the cup. For anyone who eats and drinks without recognizing the body of the Lord eats and drinks judgment on himself. **1 Corinthians 11:28-29**

When my wife and I go on vacation, we always take photos to help us remember the things we see and do. Some of the most precious things we lost when our home was flooded in Hurricane Katrina were our pictures. The albums we had from the past were destroyed in the floodwaters, and there is no way to get them back.

When Jesus was preparing for His crucifixion, He wanted to give His people a picture that would remind them of what this new covenant was all about. In the absence of photos, God has given us two ways to remember our new covenant with Him: baptism and the Lord's Supper. These are visual illustrations that remind us of what Christ has done in our lives. They represent the meaning of the new covenant. As a result, these pictures are very important in the Church.

This week, we'll study from 1 Corinthians 11. The Corinthians had been abusing the Lord's Supper. They needed to be reminded of how important it was. I think the same thing is often true today. We participate in the Lord's Supper, but we're not always sure why it's so significant. Let's study this passage this week and ask God to help us understand why this picture is so important in the Church.

Day 1 >

1 Corinthians 11:17-22;
John 13:35

Read 1 Corinthians 11:17-22. To understand these verses, you need to know that the Church would have a big meal before taking the Lord's Supper. In Corinth, these dinners had become divisive; the rich would eat most of the food leaving the poor with little to eat.

Paul told them that needed to stop. The purpose of the Lord's Supper is to bring the Church together as one Body to celebrate what Christ has done for us. In their celebration of the Lord's Supper, the Corinthians were forgetting what Jesus had taught his disciples in John 13:35 at the first Lord's Supper: to love one another!

Journal today about the importance of unity among Christians. Do you have cliques in your youth group that keep the group from being unified? What can you do to bring greater unity among the students at your church? Pray for unity in your church that can only come when you love one another.

Day 2 >>

1 Corinthians 11:23-24;
Exodus 12:1-30

After reading 1 Corinthians 11:23, read Exodus 12:1-30. The night Jesus was betrayed was during the Passover celebration.

Understanding the Passover feast is important to understanding the Lord's Supper. The Passover was designed by God to show how He had saved His people through the blood of a Lamb during the Exodus.

When we take the Lord's Supper, we're participating in a remembrance that not only goes back to what Jesus did on the cross but also goes all the way back to the beginning of the Old Testament. We are celebrating the fact that God has always been faithful to provide for His people's salvation!

Being in covenant with God means that we are constantly aware of His faithfulness to us. How has He been faithful to you this week? Journal about the evidence of God's faithfulness in your life, and praise Him for providing everything you need, especially your salvation!

Day 3 >>>
1 Corinthians 11:23-25; Ephesians 2:11-13

Read 1 Corinthians 11:23-25. As we continue to study the Lord's Supper, we see that the bread and the cup were symbols of the body and the blood of Christ. As we read Paul's words about the Lord's Supper, we learn that this is a symbol for us to remember what Christ has done.

We have already been forgiven of our sins by what Christ did on the cross with

His body and His blood. We don't have to physically do something in order to receive this forgiveness. We have the Lord's Supper as a symbol of what has already been done for us by the body and blood of Christ.

Read Ephesians 2:11-13, which talks about how we have been brought into this covenant that the Lord's Supper symbolizes. Begin journaling about why you think the Lord's Supper is so important. Why is it important for us to be constantly reminded of the new covenant we have with God in Christ?

Day 4 >>>>
1 Corinthians 11:26;
Matthew 26:26-29

Read 1 Corinthians 11:26 and Matthew 26:26-29. Notice two important things. First, Jesus is coming back. The Lord's Supper is not just a celebration of what Jesus did in the past. Jesus promised His disciples He would have a meal with them again in the future. He promised to come back for His people!

In light of this (and this is the second point), Paul reminded Christians to proclaim the death of Christ until He returns. We have the responsibility to tell as many people as possible about the love and sacrifice of Christ. We should be active in proclaiming the Lord's death until He comes back!

When was the last time you shared the love and sacrifice of Christ with someone else? Journal today about what it means to have this responsibility. Then commit to sharing the love and sacrifice of Christ with someone this week. Pray that God will use you to lead someone to place their faith in Christ for the first time this week.

Day 5 >>>>>
1 Corinthians 11:27-34; Luke 22:14-20

We've seen how important the Lord's Supper is. But how should we take the it? Do we just come in, eat the bread, drink from the cup, and call it a day? The Bible says Paul said no. We have to examine ourselves before taking the Lord's Supper.

The Christians in Corinth had started treating the Lord's Supper like it was no big deal. Before partaking in the Lord's Supper, they needed to search their hearts to see if there was anything displeasing to God. They couldn't take the Lord's Supper and celebrate the forgiveness of Christ if they were deliberately disobeying God.

Journal today about what you need to do before the next time you take the Lord's Supper in church. How can you prepare yourself? Search your heart today to see if anything in your life is not pleasing to Him, ask Him to forgive you of your sins, and surrender your life today to living as a picture of His love and grace.

The Perfect Ending

I read about a Hollywood wedding not too long ago: 300 guests, approximately 30,000 roses, and about a million dollars spent total. Food was flown in from 14 different countries. More than 200 pounds of shrimp, lobster, and crab were served. If you do the math, that's two pounds of seafood for every guest. They had 2,000 pounds of tomatoes, 4,300 cups of coffee, 1,100 cloth napkins, and a variety of other foods. It was quite a spread.

This week, we'll see the Bible's description of the ultimate wedding banquet. Our tendency is to picture an elaborate scene like the one I just mentioned. But remember the whole point of the wedding banquet. It really didn't matter to me if my wedding cost $10 or $10 million as long as my wife was there. What would you think if I showed up at my wedding and turned to you and said, "You know, I don't care if my bride shows up; I just hope the cake is good!" That's ridiculous, right? But that's how we sometimes think about heaven. We try to imagine all of the things that will be there. The main point is that we're going to be with God, with Christ, forever!

So let's dive into Revelation 19. There we'll see a picture of the wedding banquet that we're going to get to be a part of when we are united with Christ in the culmination of our covenant with God.

Revelation 19:6; Psalm 93

Read Revelation 19:6. Can you picture this happening? Can you imagine the sound … a huge multitude of people shouting so loud it sounds like rushing waters and thunder? And the first word out of their mouths is, "Hallelujah," which means, "Praise the Lord!" What an amazing scene!

Read Psalm 93. These verses are similar to the song we might imagine will be sung on that day. All of God's people will sing praise to Him. He is sovereign and in control of all things. He is the King of the universe who has all power in heaven and on earth. He is our King!

Begin this week in your journal by writing out a song of praise. You don't have to be a skilled songwriter. Just write out a prayer that expresses adoration and praise to God. And as you write, imagine the day when you will truly sing that song in His presence!

Revelation 19:7; Revelation 18:1-3

Before Revelation 19:7, John paints a picture of the sinfulness of people who disobeyed God. Read Revelation 18:1-3 to get a picture of the spiritual adultery that was bringing destruction to people. Those who disobey God and have not trusted in Him will experience the horrible consequences of their sin.

Now read Revelation 19:7. The picture is not evil and filth but beauty and purity. Here in Revelation, we are seeing two pictures: one of the judgment of God and one of the mercy of God. The judgment of God leads to the eternal consequences of sin, but the mercy of God leads to the eternal joy of forgiveness.

Journal about how your actions today affect your life for eternity. For example, what can you do now to make yourself ready for the day when you will meet Christ? Ask God to make you more pure each day as you await the time when you will come face to face with Him.

Day 3 >>>

Revelation 19:7; Luke 14:15-24

Read and memorize Revelation 19:7. Throughout the New Testament, the Bible refers to the Church as the bride of Christ. When Revelation 19:7 talks about a bride who is ready to meet her husband, this is talking about you and me!

Read Luke 14:15-24. Jesus talks about a parable of a great banquet. We are invited to this banquet, not because we deserve it, but because of grace. The King of the universe invites us to eat at His table and enjoy His presence forever.

One thing to remember is that the King is inviting more people to the table. He wants to draw more people to Christ. This is why sharing the love of this King is the most important thing we can do. Who can you share the Gospel with today? Pray that God will use you to extend His invitation of grace to others so that they might become a part of the bride of Christ.

Day 4 >>>>
Revelation 19:8;
Revelation 21:18-21

Brides are usually dressed in beautiful white dresses. You don't see brides wearing black. Why not? Because white symbolizes the purity and goodness of the bride. In Revelation 19:8, the bride is dressed in complete purity. She is wearing the finest clothes, as white as you can imagine.

The picture becomes even more complete in Revelation 21:18-21. Heaven is depicted as a beautiful place where the bride of Christ's purity reflects His purity. The result is a perfect portrait of many colors reflecting the purity of you and me.

This is a wonderful ending to the Bible. What started with the fall of man ends with men and women purified by the blood of Christ. As you journal today, write about the areas of your life that are pure as well as the areas of your life that need to be made more pure. Confess any impurity to Him, and ask Him to make you pure by His grace.

Day 5 >>>>>>

Revelation 19:6-9;
Revelation 12:10-12

This passage closes with John hearing how blessed the people are who are invited to this wedding banquet. The people in John's day were facing a lot of temptation to turn away from Christ. They were being persecuted and many of them were suffering for their faith.

Read Revelation 12:10-12. These people overcame their difficulties and trusted in Christ. As a result, they knew that one day they would be at this wedding banquet. And any type of persecution or suffering was worth enduring to know they would be united with Christ as His bride.

Journal today about how this picture in Revelation 19:6-9 brings encouragement to your faith. How does the anticipation of that day help you face trials and difficult times in this world? Ask God to give you strength today to endure whatever life brings you because one day you will be united with Him forever.

The Marriage Covenant

memory verse

The LORD God said, "It is not good for the man to be alone. I will make a helper suitable for him." **Genesis 2:18**

The subject of dating brings up all kinds of discussion among students today. People say you date to have fun, for social reasons, for spiritual reasons, to prepare for the person you are going to marry, and so on. And in the middle of it all, some people say you shouldn't date, period.

If you are going to date, whom should you date? And how? Do Christians date the same way non-Christians date? What are the dangers we should avoid when we think about dating? Many times during our study of covenant, we have seen marriage as a good illustration of our covenant with God. This is the way God designed it. This has huge implications for how we look at the dating process. No matter what you think the purpose of dating is, you will most likely end up marrying someone you have dated. So how can our dating relationships reflect our covenant with God?

Let's see what the Bible says about the marriage covenant. And along the way, we'll understand God's design for a guy and a girl when they come together in marriage. As a result, we'll know how to live our lives so that we make the most of marriage the way God designed it to be.

Day 1 >

Genesis 2:18; Proverbs 3:5-6

Read Genesis 2:18. God's love is evident from the very beginning of this passage. From the start, we see that God desires the best for His creation. He saw that the man was alone, and this was not good.

As you begin to think about dating and marriage, remember that God knows exactly what is good for us. Sometimes we live in our dating relationships like we don't really believe this. Does God really know what is best for us in dating and marriage? The Bible says, "yes." If you need another reminder of this, check out Proverbs 3:5-6.

Journal about what you believe God desires for dating relationships, and eventually, marriage. What do you think is "best" in God's eyes? Feel free to examine other Scriptures to support your thoughts. Pray today that God will help you to trust what He says is best in this area of your life.

Day 2 >>

Genesis 2:19-20; Proverbs 2:16-19

Genesis 2:20 says that "no suitable helper" was found for Adam. God saw that Adam needed a partner who would walk with him through life. God was going to establish not only a covenant between Himself and man but also God a covenant between

covenant: Knowing God—His Relationship with His People

man and woman as partners in His creation.

From this early point in Scripture, throughout the rest of the Old Testament and into the New Testament, the importance of the partnership (or marriage covenant) between man and woman is constantly talked about. Look over in Proverbs 2:16-19. Because of how important the marriage covenant is, the writer warned people not to leave that bond.

As you journal today, think about the significance of the marriage covenant. Why do you think marriage is important? What do you think the Bible means when it talks about the man and woman helping each other?

Day 3 >>>

Genesis 2:15-20;
Hebrews 10:23-25

Read Genesis 2:15. God put man in the garden to work the ground and to worship and obey Him. When God gave man a helper, He was giving man someone who would help him worship and obey God.

God designed marriage to be a relationship in which a man and woman help one another worship and obey God. It's the kind of picture we see later in Hebrews 10:23-25, where people are spurring one another on toward God. The marriage relationship is designed so that a man helps his wife love and serve God and a woman helps her husband worship and obey Him.

What do you think this means for dating relationships? Journal today about how a dating relationship could either draw you closer to God or take you further from God. Pray today that God would use the relationships you have with others to draw you closer to Him and not further away.

Day 4 >>>>

Genesis 2:21-23; Genesis 1:26-28

Read Genesis 2:21-23 and Genesis 1:26-28. Among all the creatures on the earth, only man and woman were made in the image of God. Today, we have the responsibility of reflecting God's image in all of creation. That's why Genesis 1:28 says to be fruitful and multiply.

But remember that in Genesis 3, this image was marred by sin. As a result, the image of God is distorted in our lives. Thankfully, though, we know the rest of the story. Jesus died to forgive us of our sins so that we could be made complete in Christ.

How important do you believe the presence of Jesus is in a marriage? When two imperfect people come together, is Jesus necessary for them to experience what God designed for marriage? As you journal today, write about the importance of having Jesus at the center of a marriage and at the center of a dating relationship. How can you keep Jesus at the center?

Day 5 >>>>>

Genesis 2:24;
1 Corinthians 6:18-20

Genesis 2:24 is often quoted at weddings as it summarizes the picture of marriage the way God designed it. Marriage is much more than a social relationship. It is a spiritual and physical uniting of two lives to worship and obey God with all their hearts.

This importance of physically uniting comes up throughout the Bible. Check out 1 Corinthians 6:18-20. God's people were commanded to honor Him with their bodies. Our bodies are designed to be united in a spiritual and physical relationship with someone in marriage. Yet our culture tempts males and females to forget this and to give their bodies to people they are not married to. When this happens, we miss out on what God has designed for us.

Journal today about the importance of honoring God with your body, particularly in a dating or marriage relationship. Are you honoring God with your body? Pray today that God will help you to be pure and holy as you face temptations to miss out on what is God's best for you.

Unending Love

memory verse

"Daughters of Jerusalem, I charge you: Do not arouse or awaken love until it so desires." **Song of Songs 8:4**

Have you ever heard kids share their thoughts on a topic? It can be humorous. A while ago, I came across some quotes from children on the subject of love. They were hilarious! To hear these kids talk about marriage, love, husbands and wives . . . I laughed so hard at how messed up these kids' views on love were. But then I realized that many of us also have a hard time figuring out love. To be such an important concept, it can be a confusing thing.

Whether we are five years old or 85, love, romance and marriage are topics that are important to us. Sometimes we get the idea that love and romance aren't important parts of the Bible.

Does God really talk about what romance looks like? Absolutely!

This subject comes up in many places in the Bible, but most completely in the Book of Song of Songs. This book is filled with descriptions of love between a man and a woman. This week, we're going to dive into what many have called one of the greatest descriptions of love in written history. It's a picture of romance between a man and a woman who are experiencing love the way God designed it to be. Let's get a glimpse of this kind of love and ask God to help us experience love the way He designed it to be.

Day 1 >

Song of Songs 8:1-3; 1 Corinthians 13:1-3

As you read Song of Songs 8:1-3, you see a man and woman walking together outside. She expresses her love to him as she describes how he holds her in his arms. Wow! Some of us didn't even know the Bible talks like this!

God has given us the desire for a man or woman in marriage. My desire for my wife is a God-given desire. It's not a bad thing; in fact, it's a blessed thing! God has blessed us with desires for love and romance. These desires only become bad when we abuse them and use them in a context outside of what God has designed.

How can you make sure the desire God gives you for a member of the opposite sex brings honor to Him? Journal today about how God wants to bless that desire in you. Thank Him for the gift of love and romance.

Day 2 >>

Song of Songs 8:1-3; 1 Corinthians 13:1-3

As we read Song of Songs 8:1-3 again today, we need to see what the New Testament teaches us about love. Read 1 Corinthians 13:1-3. Notice the importance God is placing on love.

Without love, even faith that moves mountains is meaningless!

First Corinthians 13 is talking about love in more than a marriage sense. But it is still helpful in understanding what love looks like. Marriage does not just involve love for one other person. It's also love for God. When two people who love God with all their hearts come together, they are able to love each other in a way that brings honor to God.

How does your love for God affect the way you act in dating relationships as you prepare for marriage? Journal today about how your love for God is the foundation of your love for others. Ask God to help you honor Him today by the way you love the people around you.

Day 3 >>>

Song of Songs 8:4; 1 Corinthians 13:4-6

Song of Songs 8:4 is the memory verse for this week. This woman was experiencing the joy of love the way God designed it. She gave the women around her this piece of advice: "Do not arouse or awaken love until it so desires." This is very similar to the description of love in 1 Corinthians 13:4-6: "Love is patient . . ."

When you enter into a relationship with someone of the opposite sex, your emotions

may run wild. The result is that you begin showing love to that person. This is the way a marriage is designed to be. There's just one problem: You're not married yet! God's will for you is to save this kind of love for your husband or wife.

In your words, what does it mean to be patient with love. How can you keep from awakening love until the proper time? How can you save your love for the person God gives you to marry? Ask God to help you be patient with love.

Day 4 >>>>

Song of Songs 8:5-7; 1 Corinthians 13:7

Song of Songs 8:5-7 teaches that love never fades or ends. First Corinthians 13:7 is similar. Notice Paul uses the word "always" four times to stress the point that love never fails. Marriage love is a strong tie between two people that should never be broken.

This is why wedding vows usually say, "until death do us part." God's design for love is that it will never be broken by anything of this earth. This kind of love can come only from God and is reserved for marriage. He is infinitely loving. He is the ultimate source of unconditional love. So when a man and woman come together in marriage, they need God's love as the foundation for their love for one another.

Journal today about the strength of God's love for you. What does it mean for God to love you unconditionally? How does marriage reflect this kind of unconditional love? Thank God today for the unconditional love He has given you.

Day 5 >>>>>>

Song of Songs 8:5-7; 1 Corinthians 13:8-13

In Song of Songs 8:6, we read about the "jealousy" of love. Just as God is jealous for our love, it is right for a woman to be jealous for the love of her husband and for a man to be jealous for the love of his wife. I know this is true in my own marriage. I don't want my wife loving any other guys. I want all of her love!

Just as a marriage requires complete and total love given to another person, the same is true in our covenant relationship with God. I am supposed to love my wife exclusively. I am also supposed to love God exclusively. When this happens, the marriage covenant is an incredible picture of our relationship with God!

Journal today about your own love for God. Is it exclusive? Or have you divided your love between God and other things? Pray today that you will learn to love God wholeheartedly as you prepare to love your husband or wife in the future.

covenant: Knowing God—His Relationship with His People

Being Faithful

Have we not all one Father? Did not one God create us? Why do we profane the covenant of our fathers by breaking faith with one another?

Malachi 2:10

I remember struggling with the idea of love when my wife, Heather, and I were dating. We didn't want to say, "I love you," to each other until we really knew what that meant.

So we decided we weren't going to say, "I love you," to each other—or anyone else we might date in the future—until we were ready to commit completely to that other person. This way, we could reserve the love God designed for a marriage relationship for the person God called us to marry. On the night we got engaged, I got down on my knee and told her I loved her for the first time. And when I used the word love, I meant it. I was committed to loving her for the rest of my life.

We're going to see in Scripture this week that love in dating and marriage should not be taken lightly. Love is a huge commitment. And that's the way God designed it. He made a huge commitment to love us when He sent His only Son to die on a cross. This is total love, and marriage is supposed to be a reflection of this kind of love.

Many of us come from homes where the marriage covenant has been broken. And even if your parents have kept their marriage covenant, there's still a lot of pressure on all of us to cheapen love and break the commitment that this kind of love involves. Let's dive in and see what God's perspective is on the importance of love in the marriage covenant.

Malachi 2:10-11;
2 Corinthians 6:14-7:1

In Malachi 2:10-11, God expresses His displeasure at the men of Israel. They had married foreigners who worshiped foreign gods. The women pulled the men away from God. In 2 Corinthians 6:14-7:1, God warns us not to have relationships like this with unbelievers because they will pull us away from devotion to God.

I think the Bible is clearly telling us that we should not date unbelievers. I want to encourage you to begin thinking about why it's important to have someone close to you who is also pursuing God with all of his or her heart.

Journal today about someone in your life who helps you grow in your relationship with God. How does this person encourage you in your pursuit of Christ? Then pray that God will provide someone for you to marry who will do the same thing . . . someone who will spur you on to love Christ with everything you have.

Day 2 >>

Malachi 2:13-14;
1 Corinthians 10:31-33

In Malachi 2:13-14, God talks about how the people would bring God offerings of worship, yet they wouldn't love their spouses. Malachi says they're going to experience the judgment of God because they have not loved their wives or husbands.

The marriage covenant is designed to be a reflection of our worship and love of God. When I love my wife like God commands me, I am showing love for God at the same time. That's exactly why 1 Corinthians 10:31-33 says what it does. We are supposed to bring God glory with every single thing we do, including the way we honor the marriage covenant.

As you journal today, think about how this affects your perspective of dating. How can you worship God through the way you date? List at least five ways you can worship God through your dating relationships, and then pray that God will be honored in you through the way you date.

Day 3 >>>
Malachi 2:13-14; Isaiah 62:1-5

God wants us to experience satisfaction—spiritually, emotionally, and physically—within marriage. Read Isaiah 62:1-5. What an incredible picture of the joy and delight we can know when we experience love the way God has designed it!

But the other side of the picture is Malachi 2:13-14. When we disobey God and break the marriage covenant, we miss out on His blessings. The consequences are great; these verses talk about the people weeping and wailing. God had withdrawn His blessing from them because they had been unfaithful in their marriages.

As you journal today, begin by thinking about three ways God blesses marriages. Then write about three consequences of the marriage covenant being broken. Ask God to lead and guide you so that one day you will experience the fullness of His blessings in marriage.

Day 4 >>>>

Malachi 2:15; Matthew 19:3-9

Read Malachi 2:15 and Matthew 19:3-9, and it quickly becomes obvious: God doesn't want the marriage covenant broken. God tells His people to guard themselves so that they keep the marriage covenant at all times.

Why is this so important to God? The answer is simple: He promises to keep His covenant with us. If the marriage covenant is a picture, or illustration, of God's covenant with us, then it should never be broken. God wants His unconditional love to be reflected in the love between a husband and wife.

As you journal today, start by memorizing Malachi 2:10 and then writing it out without looking at your Bible. Then write a prayer asking God to help you guard

covenant: Knowing God—His Relationship with His People

your heart as you date (and one day marry) so that His covenant is reflected in the way you love your husband or wife.

Day 5 >>>>>
Malachi 2:16; Hebrews 13:4

Read Malachi 2:16. God actually says, "I hate divorce." Strong words, right? We shouldn't be surprised. Dating and marriage are extremely important to God. When we disobey and dishonor Him in these areas, He promises we will miss out on His blessings. That's why Hebrews 13:4 warns us to keep the marriage bed pure.

Divorce is not a part of God's design for marriage. But because of human sinfulness, nearly half of American marriages end in divorce. Thankfully, the God who hates divorce is also the God who desires to bring forgiveness and healing. He is always faithful to keep His covenant of love with His children.

If your parents are divorced, spend some time journaling about how this has affected your life. Then spend some time praying for your parents. On the other hand, if your parents are not divorced, pray for someone you know who is in that situation. Ask God to bring healing and forgiveness in their lives through the love of Christ.

The Intention of the Marriage Covenant

memory verse

"So they are no longer two, but one. Therefore what God has joined together, let man not separate."
Matthew 19:6

Should a Christian date a non-Christian? I think of it this way: When we ask if it's okay to date a non-Christian, we are assuming that God's best is not possible for us. Now, some people will say: "I want to date a non-Christian so I can lead them to Christ." I say the best way to show Christ to others is to show them that Christ is more important to us than anyone in this world—nothing could pull us away from Him. That's a great way to witness!

My advice is to not date non-Christians and to not date just those who are Christians. I would say to date only growing Christians. I would challenge you to only pursue a dating relationship with someone who is also pursuing Christ. I picture it like a race. You are running after Jesus as hard as you can. Along the way, look beside you to see who else is running after Him. If you see somebody you'd like to date, invite him or her to run with you! I believe this is what the

Bible teaches when it comes to dating in preparation for marriage.

This week, we'll continue to think about the marriage covenant and how it mirrors God's covenant with us. We'll learn how He wants to unite us with someone who is passion- ately pursuing God and fleeing sin in their lives. We're going to see how physical impurity can destroy a marriage and lead to divorce. Let's take a closer look.

covenant: Knowing God—His Relationship with His People

Day 1 >

Matthew 19:3; Mark 10:1-12

Read Matthew 19:3. The Jewish culture was teaching that divorce was okay in just about any circumstance. If a husband looked at a woman who wasn't his wife, his wife could divorce him. If the wife cooked a bad meal for the husband, he could divorce her! Ouch!

Now read Mark 10:1-12. Today, a lot of people don't really know what the Bible teaches about divorce. We have to ask the question: "What's more important to us: what Jesus says about divorce or what our culture teaches us about divorce?" Many people don't think divorce is a very important issue. Are we willing to really listen to what Jesus says, even if it goes against what the rest of our culture says?

As you journal today, write about what you think our culture says about divorce. Then write about what God says about divorce. Pray that God will help us to understand His perspective on this important issue this week.

Day 2 >>

Matthew 19:4-5; Genesis 2:24

The Pharisees were trying to find a reason for divorce. Jesus responded by quoting from Genesis 2:24. He reminded them (and us) that God ordains for a man and woman to stay together in marriage. That's the way

God intended marriage. Anytime we go against this design, we are missing out on marriage the way God planned it to be.

Marriage is the perfect unity between a woman and a man. You are too young to consider marriage. But as you grow older, the people you date will be potential marriage partners. In order to eventually experience this perfect unity, your goal is to date people who desire Jesus Christ above all else.

Journal today about the kind of person you would like to marry. What does that person look like? (Not just physically, but spiritually and emotionally.) What characteristics does the person have? Pray that God will give you strength not to settle for less than His best for you.

Day 3 >>>

Matthew 19:4-6; Genesis 1:26-28

As you look back over Matthew 19:4-6, Jesus was talking about the importance of physical union in marriage. He spoke about how a male and a female come together as one "flesh." This goes back to Genesis 1:26-28. God created us as physical creatures, male and female. This physical unity is obviously very important to Christ's understanding of marriage.

And this is why physical purity in dating relationships is so important. God desires for us to save our physical bodies so that, one day, we will unite our body together with the person He gives us to marry.

Journal today about the importance of saving your physical body completely for the person you will marry one day. Pray that God will give you strength to be physically pure in every relationship you have in order to prepare for marriage.

Day 4 >>>>
Matthew 19:7-8; Deuteronomy 24:1-4

Read Matthew 19:7-8. The Pharisees questioned Jesus about what Moses said in the Old Testament. Now read Deuteronomy 24:1-4. Moses permitted divorce in certain circumstances. But notice how the Pharisees phrased the question; they said Moses commanded the people to divorce. Jesus points out that divorce is never commanded in God's Word. Instead, Moses allowed it.

Matthew 19:8 says Moses allowed divorce because the people's hearts were hard. They had fallen into sin and had disobeyed God. Divorce is not part of God's plan. He designed marriage as a lasting covenant between man and woman. We have divorce because our hearts are sinful and problems arise in a marriage as a result.

Journal today about how you can avoid dishonoring God in dating relationships (even one day in a marriage relationship). The root of divorce is sin. Pray that God will help you to flee sin and pursue Him with all your heart.

Day 5 >>>>>>

Matthew 19:9;
1 Thessalonians 4:3-8

Matthew 19:9 gives one reason divorce should be permitted. The word Jesus used translates "marital unfaithfulness" and refers mainly to adultery. In other words, divorce is permitted when a man or woman breaks the marriage covenant in this horrible way.

The rest of the New Testament shows us the devastation that accompanies physical sin and impurity. Read 1 Thessalonians 4:3-8. This passage warns us to flee sexual immorality. Physical sin like this dishonors God. It also dishonors what God intends for the physical unity in a marriage relationship.

Journal today about any struggles you have had with physical purity. What steps can you take in your life to avoid sexual immorality, as 1 Thessalonians 4:3-8 says? Pray that God will provide a person in your life to hold you accountable to physical purity, and then ask that person this week if they would be willing to do that for you.

A Reflection of Christ and the Church

memory verse

Husbands, love your wives, just as Christ loved the church and gave himself up for her. **Ephesians 5:25**

Guys, here are some tips for when you get engaged. First, start saving now! Yes, the bride's family will probably pay for the wedding. But you'll be paying for the ring. Those things aren't cheap. Start saving early!

Second, there are two words to remember: "Yes, dear." Whenever your future bride asks if you would do something, you just say, "Yes, dear." Don't hesitate, don't pause. Right away, do whatever she says!

Finally, remember one very important truth: It's not about you! During your engagement, people are going to be throwing her a lot of parties. You will not be invited to most of them. When your wedding day comes, people are there to see the bride. Not you. It's a hard truth, but it helps to learn it now.

This week, we'll finish our examination of the marriage covenant with some Scripture regarding marriage. We'll read about wives submitting to their husbands and husbands sacrificing for their wives. What does this mean? The point is that it's not about us. It's about laying down our lives to honor a husband or a wife and, ultimately, to honor Christ. This passage is significant as we prepare for marriage one day. So let's dive into Ephesians 5 and see what submission and sacrifice are all about.

Day 1 >

Ephesians 5:21; Galatians 5:13-15

Read Ephesians 5:21. The Bible says "submit to one another out of reverence for Christ." When the Bible uses this word "submit," it is not saying we should devalue or demean ourselves. It's saying God puts us in different positions, and we should simply respect one another.

In Galatians 5:13-15, Paul talked about serving each other. He was talking about how we should respect civil authorities, church leaders, and our parents. By serving people in these types of positions, we bring glory to Christ.

Journal today about what it means to submit to someone else or to serve them. Write one thing you can do to go out of your way to serve someone else. Pray that Christ will be honored in the way you serve that person, and then do it out of reverence for Christ.

Day 2 >>

Ephesians 5:22-33;
1 Corinthians 11:3

Read Ephesians 5:22-33. Notice the roles men and women have in marriage. This passage becomes controversial only when people think, "The Bible is saying men are superior to women!" That's not what the Bible is saying at all.

Read 1 Corinthians 11:3. This passage deals with man as the head of the woman and God as the head of Christ. Ask yourself: Is God greater than Christ? No. We know Christ is fully God. They are equal with one another. But the Bible teaches that Christ and God have different roles. Similarly, man is not superior to woman. They simply have different roles. Remember: The point of marriage is to reflect the character and covenant of God.

Think about God the Father and God the Son. How does the Bible say they relate to one another? Now think about a husband and wife. How does the Bible say they relate to one another? Ask God to help you understand the different roles of men and women in marriage this week.

Day 3 >>>

Ephesians 5:22-24;
Colossians 3:15-21

Read Ephesians 5:22-24. Notice the wife's role. Wives are to submit to their husbands. Now read Colossians 3:15-21. Notice a similar command? Like we saw on the first day of this week, the idea of submission means that a woman serves her husband out of reverence for Christ.

No woman should be a slave to her husband, forced to do everything he says. That's not the picture the Bible is painting. Instead, this word for submission literally means "voluntary service." A wife desires to honor her husband and serve him, not because she has to, but because she loves him.

Girls, what kind of guy is worth serving—not because you have to but because you want to? Record your thoughts. Guys, what kind of girl will display this kind of servant spirit to those around her? Record your thoughts. Pray that God would give us all servant spirits and lead us to people who have the desire to serve each other.

Day 4 >>>>
Ephesians 5:25-28; 1 John 3:16-18

I realize some of you were a bit uneasy as you read yesterday's devotion. This talk about a woman serving a man doesn't seem right if that's all the Bible says. But guess what? That's not the whole story.

Husbands are commanded to love their wives and sacrifice their lives for them, just like Christ did for the Church. A woman would willingly serve a guy who would sacrifice his life for her. It's the same with the Church. We don't think it's a burden to serve Christ, because He laid down His life for us.

Girls, describe the characteristics of a guy who would sacrifice all for you. Guys, journal today about what you need to do in order to sacrifice your life to serve those around you. Guys and girls, pray that God will prepare you for your future husband or wife.

Day 5 »»»»»

Ephesians 5:29-33; Revelation 21:1-5

Read Ephesians 5:29-33. Here, Paul talked about a husband caring for his wife as he would his own body. This kind of care involves a lot of responsibility. A godly husband cares for his wife physically, spiritually, and emotionally.

Read Revelation 21:1-5. Christ will be united with His bride, the Church (that's us!). He cleanses us from our sins and prepares us for eternity. If this is what awaits us, we want to find a husband or a wife who will encourage us to love Christ so we will be ready on that day.

Throughout our study of the marriage covenant, we've seen that God desires to bless us with marriage. As we finish, write a prayer to God that expresses your desire to do whatever it takes to be the man or woman Christ calls you to be. Then close by thanking Him for the beauty of marriage that reflects the beauty of His covenant with us.

David's Words

On January 8, 1956, five men—Jim Elliot, Pete Fleming, Ed McCully, Nate Saint, and Roger Youderian—met with a dangerous Ecuadorian tribe, the Aucas. They had each left promising careers in the United States and moved with their families to Ecuador to be missionaries. The Aucas suddenly attacked the five men. Within minutes, each man was dead.

Shortly before these missionaries were attacked and killed, they were reported to have sung a song: "We rest on Thee, our Shield and our Defender, We go not forth alone against the foe. Strong in Thy strength, safe in Thy keeping tender, we rest on Thee, and in Thy name we go." These last words summarize the commitment of these men. They expressed their confidence in God's provision, and they surrendered to go wherever God led them, even if that meant death.

This week, we're going to look at 2 Samuel 23:1-7, a passage that contains the last words of King David. And though David did not die a martyr's death, we're going to see the same kind of confidence in David that these men had in Ecuador on the day they died. Throughout history, God has proven to be faithful to those who trust in Him. That same support is available for you and me today. So let's see David's last words in the Bible and see how, even as he was dying, he was confident in the covenant God had made with him.

2 Samuel 23:1; Luke 18:14

As you read 2 Samuel 23:1, notice how David said that God was the One who had exalted him, and God was the One who had anointed him. David knew he was king in Israel and had experienced the blessings of God only because God had been faithful to him.

This is the major difference between David and the king who served before him, Saul. Saul tried to exalt himself and ended up falling into evil, but David humbled himself and let God bring honor to him. This is exactly what Jesus taught in Luke 18:14. When we humble ourselves before God, He will exalt us in a way that He receives glory and praise.

What does it mean to humble yourself? Journal today about how you can be more humble. And pray that God will increase your humility so He might be exalted in your life.

2 Samuel 23:2; Acts 1:8

Read 2 Samuel 23:2. When the Spirit of the Lord was on David, the Spirit spoke through him and put God's words on his tongue. This is one of the common features of the Holy Spirit that we see in the Bible. When the Spirit of God is on people, they are often speaking the Word of God. Read Acts 1:8. Jesus told His disciples that the Holy Spirit would come upon them and they would be witnesses. When the Holy Spirit is in us, not only do our lives honor Christ, but we also speak the Word of God. In other words, we tell other people about Christ!

Who can you verbally share the love of Christ with today? Journal and pray today that the Holy Spirit would put God's Word on your tongue—just as He did with David—so that you will have strength to speak about the Gospel today with someone else.

Day 3 >>>

2 Samuel 23:3-4; Matthew 5:16

David wasn't perfect. He sinned against God and experienced the consequences of sin. But throughout his life, David strived for righteousness. He desired to honor God with the way he ruled the people of Israel. Read 2 Samuel 23:3-4. At the end of his life, David stated that when you live righteously, you shine like the sun on a clear morning.

Read Matthew 5:16. Jesus said to let the light of His righteousness shine in us so that people may see our lives and give glory to God. We have opportunities to shine His light every day with the way we live.

covenant: Knowing God—His Relationship with His People

Journal today about what you can do to shine the love and righteousness of Christ. Write three practical things you can do and then pray that God will use your life today to shine so others may see the greatness of God through you.

Day 4 >>>>

2 Samuel 23:5; Genesis 9:16

In Samuel 23:5, David spoke about the covenant God had established with him. Notice how David described this covenant. It is everlasting, secure, and guaranteed to bring him salvation. This is similar language to how Noah described God's covenant in Genesis 9:16. Just as God was faithful to His covenant with Noah, Abraham, and others, He showed the same faithfulness to David.

God's faithfulness didn't stop with David. He has promised to show you and me the same faithfulness. Our covenant with Him is everlasting, secure, and guaranteed for our salvation. In fact, Jesus gave His life to establish the new covenant with us!

Praise God today for His faithfulness to David and to you. Journal about ways God has shown His faithfulness to you this week. How can you display faithfulness to Him?

Day 5 >>>>>>

2 Samuel 23:6-7; Psalm 1

Read 2 Samuel 23:6-7. As David came to the last part of this passage, he contrasted the life he had in covenant with God with the lives of men who had turned against God. The light of the righteousness of God shines brilliantly, but the evil man is marked by darkness and death.

Read Psalm 1. Do you see the contrast between the man who trusts in God and the wicked man who doesn't follow God? The result of obedience to God's covenant is blessing, but the consequence of disobedience is costly.

Examine your life today, and identify areas of obedience and disobedience in your relationship with God. Journal about your confession concerning those areas of disobedience, and then praise God for His faithfulness to forgive you by His grace.

God's Faithfulness

memory verse

"I will punish their sin with the rod, their iniquity with flogging; but I will not take my love from him, nor will I ever betray my faithfulness. I will not violate my covenant or alter what my lips have uttered." **Psalm 89:32-34**

The King of Norway, King Harald, once did the unimaginable. When he was still a prince, Harald wanted to marry one of the common people. Many were trying to keep Harald from it. But the prince was in love with this woman. So in 1968, the commoner, Sonja Haraldsen, became the Crown Princess of Norway. Today, as the Queen of Norway, she has become one of the most important members in the history of the Norwegian royal family.

We must realize that something very similar happened to you and me. One day, the King of the Universe did something unimaginable. A gap existed between this Holy King and the common people. And so He gave His Son to bridge that gap. God became a man and Jesus died on a cross—the ultimate symbol of grace. God showed His faithful love to all people who would simply trust in Him.

This week, we're going to read about God's grace and love to David. David became king because of God's grace. But we talked about how David sinned against God. This week, we'll see a clear picture of how God remains faithful to His people, even when they sin against Him. We're going to understand more clearly that God's love is based on His faithfulness, not ours. So let's dive in and explore Psalm 89, a song that pictures the constant love of God to King David and to you and me.

Day 1 >

Psalm 89:1-2; Isaiah 55:1-3

Over the next three days, we're going to be focusing on Psalm 89:1-8. Start today by underlining every time you see the word "faithfulness" in these verses. This word sets the tone for the entire Psalm. God is faithful to keep His covenant with His people. His love is constant. It never ends.

For another perspective on God's faithfulness, check out Isaiah 55:1-3. These verses talk about the satisfaction that is found in knowing God. He quenches our thirst and fulfills all our cravings because He is alone faithful to keep His covenant forever.

Throughout our study of covenant, we have talked a lot about God's faithfulness. What does it mean for God to be faithful to His people? Journal today about some of the ways God shows faithfulness to His people. Then pray that God will help you understand more clearly His faithfulness as we study Scripture this week.

Day 2 >>

Psalm 89:3-4; 1 Samuel 16:1-13

Read Psalm 89:3-4. These verses show us that God chose David to be His servant. Look back, and read 1 Samuel 16:1-13. This is the story of how God chose David to be king of His people, Israel.

Even though David wasn't the strongest or the smartest guy in his day, God poured out His grace on him. The result was that David became God's servant. He carried out God's will and obeyed God's law. David knew that He had been chosen by grace. His entire life was surrendered to serving God.

This same truth applies to you and me today. We have not received our salvation because we were the strongest or the smartest people. We are where we are today because of God's grace. We are called to be His servants, completely surrendered to following Him. What does it mean to be God's servant? Journal about specific things you can do to serve Him with all your heart.

Day 3 >>>
Psalm 89:5-8; Psalm 24:1-10

As you read Psalm 89:5-8, notice that even the heavenly beings stand in constant awe of God. He is more awesome than anything in heaven or earth. What an incredible picture of God's greatness!

Psalm 24:1-10 pictures a similar scene. Sometimes we become casual with God. When we pray to Him, sing to Him in worship, listen to His Word, we forget that we should be in constant awe of God. If the angels stand in awe, then we certainly should do the same. Sometimes we miss this.

When you pray or when you sing in church or when you read God's Word, are you in awe of Him? Journal today about how we sometimes become casual with God and forget how truly awesome He is. How can we prevent this? Spend some time today just focusing in prayer on how awesome God is.

Day 4 >>>>
Psalm 89:27-34; Deuteronomy 7:14-20

We've seen how faithful God is. But when we think about God's covenant, there are two sides to the story. Yes, God is constantly faithful. But the Bible also talks about the unfaithfulness of God's people. Read Psalm 89:27-34. Underline every time you see a disobedient action described among God's people.

Now read Deuteronomy 7:14-20. God promised to keep His covenant with David and the kings of Israel, but He also told them they were responsible for following His commands. God would not take His promise from His people, but that did not mean that they would not still receive punishment for their sins.

In light of God's faithfulness to you, journal about the responsibilities you have in covenant with Him. Then thank Him for promising not to take His love away from us.

Day 5 >>>>>

Psalm 89:35-37;
Revelation 5:1-7

We have seen over and over again in our study of covenant how what's going on in the Old Testament relates to the New Testament. Read Psalm 89:35-37. Here, you see God's promise to continue David's line forever. Did this really happen?

Turn to Revelation 5:1-7. We see Christ at the center of the throne of God. People from every nation are praising Him. Look at how He is described as "the Root of David." This is a direct link to the fact that Jesus came from the line of David. Just as God promised in Psalm 89, now we see Christ—the King of all kings from the line of David—being praised and exalted forever.

Think today about the fact that God's covenant with us will last forever. Journal about how comforting it is to know that you have eternal life through Jesus. How does that affect your life? Praise God for His faithfulness that endures forever.

Praising Him

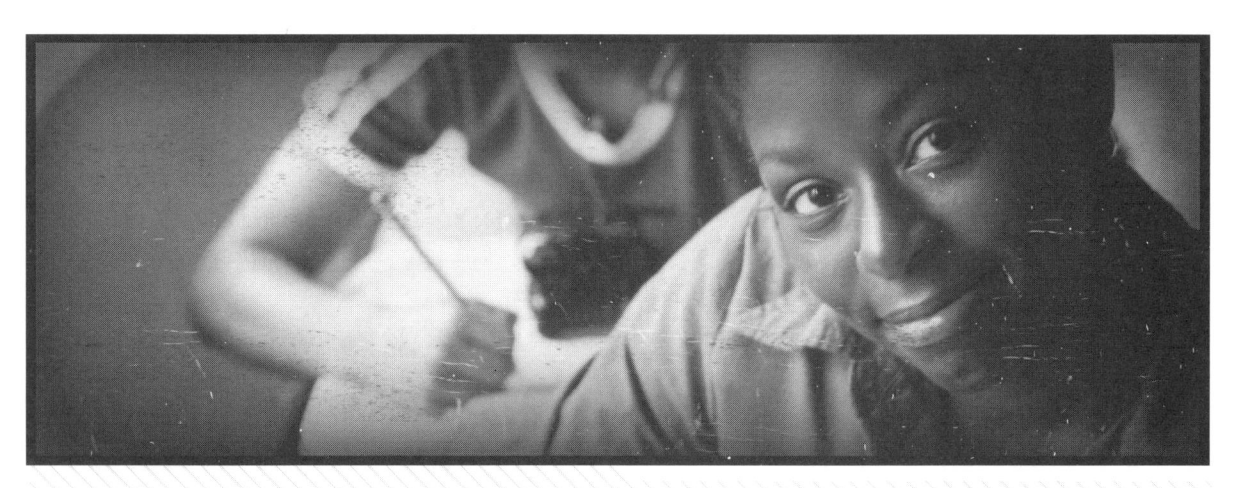

Sing to him, sing praise to him; tell of all his wonderful acts. **Psalm 105:2**

O n a trip a few years ago with some buddies of mine, I saw Steve Young, at that time, the star quarterback for the San Francisco 49ers. Acting like 10-year-old kids, we all went up to him and got his autograph and had our picture taken with him. We were pretty pumped.

Now, imagine if Steve Young had walked up to me and said, "Hey, Dave! How's it going, man? It's great to see you! When are you coming to stay at my house? We'll hang out, and then you can just go to the game with me." Well, Steve Young didn't speak to me on that day. But I have something better. The Almighty God has spoken to each of us through His Son, Jesus Christ. He sent Him to save us from our sins. He has

called us by name, according to Isaiah 43. And that's how this whole covenant thing is possible.

Now, think again about the scenario I mentioned above. What if Steve Young had said those things to me but I had ignored him? That's not a good way to respond to anybody who initiates a conversation, much less someone who's inviting you on a free trip out to San Francisco! Well, God has called our names and entered into a covenant with us. How do we respond to Him? Well, Psalm 105:1-11 gives us an answer. And as we study, we're going to see five different ways the psalmist says we should respond to God's covenant with us.

Psalm 105:1; Psalm 96:1-6

Read Psalm 105:1. Here, we see two responses to the covenant of God mentioned later in Psalm 105:8-11. The Bible tells us to give thanks to the Lord and to make known among the nations what He has done. Read Psalm 96:1-6, and you'll see a very similar command. We're told to declare God's glory among all the nations.

Did you know that over a billion people in the world today have still never heard the name of Jesus? We have work to do. Have you considered the fact that, in His covenant with you, God has commanded you to make the Gospel known in all nations? How are you committed to doing that?

As you journal today, list some of the many reasons you have to give thanks to God. Then pray that God will use you today to make known among the nations what He has done by sharing the good news of His love.

Psalm 105:2; Ephesians 5:19-20

Psalm 105:2 commands us to sing praises to God. Now, if you're like me, singing may not be your strong suit. I do enjoy singing, just so long as no one else can hear me . . . and I can't hear myself!

Read Ephesians 5:19-20. This command is apparently not just for the great singers. In response to God's love for us, He desires to hear our songs of praises to Him. So in your quiet time with God, I want to encourage you to do that. Spend some time just singing on your own. Or put on some music that expresses praise to God, and sing along. Let your voice express your praises to Him.

After you finish, journal about why you think it's important to sing praises to God. Does it help you focus your mind on who He is and what He has done for you? Why do you think singing to God is important when the church gathers together?

Day 3 >>>

Psalm 105:3; Philippians 4:4-7

As we come to Psalm 105:3, we see a third way for us to respond to God's covenant love for us. We are called to glory in God's name, which basically means to joyfully worship Him. It's the same command we see later in Philippians 4:4-7, where Paul said to rejoice in the Lord always.

Now, what does it mean to rejoice in the Lord? Does that just mean we put smiles on our faces and feel good about God? Not necessarily. To rejoice in God means we worship Him in good and bad circumstances, always confident He will take care of us no matter what happens to us.

Journal today about any difficult circumstances you have been through recently. How can you rejoice in God in those circumstances? Worship God today with the confidence that He will take care of you, no matter what happens to you.

Day 4 >>>>

Psalm 105:4; Psalm 27:1-14

Read Psalm 105:4. The psalmist gives us two commands: Look to the Lord, and seek His face always. Now read Psalm 27. Both Psalm 105:4 and Psalm 27 tell us to seek the Lord with all of our hearts because our strength is found in Him alone.

Look closely at Psalm 27:4. The psalmist said his one desire was to be in the Temple all day every day. He wanted to seek the Lord's presence at all times. Because Jesus died on the cross for us, we no longer have to go to a certain place to encounter His glory. He lives in us! We have the privilege of seeking His glory and enjoying His strength wherever we go.

As you journal, think about how you can seek the Lord in your life today? Ask God to show His strength in you as you face temptation, share the gospel, and serve the people around you.

Day 5 >>>>>

Psalm 105:5-11; Psalm 40:4-5

Psalm 105:5-11 commands us to remember what God has done in our lives. Throughout the Old Testament, God told His people to constantly remember all He had done among them so they would continue to trust Him. For an example of this, read Psalm 40:4-5.

I know this principle is true. Sometimes I have a hard time understanding what God is doing in my life. But when I go through a certain circumstance and look back, I can see that God was in control through the whole situation. He was leading me every step of the way.

Think about the last year or two in your life. Looking back, how has God shown His faithfulness to you? As you remember His work in your life today, praise Him for guiding you even when you didn't understand all that was happening. And ask Him to increase your faith in Him today as a result of what He has done in the past.

covenant: Knowing God—His Relationship with His People

Boldness in Christ

And we, who with unveiled faces all reflect the Lord's glory, are being transformed into his likeness with ever-increasing glory, which comes from the Lord, who is the Spirit.

2 Corinthians 3:18

I will never forget the group of Asian missionaries. There were about 35 of them, almost all between the ages of 15 and 25. They traveled all night to receive training in how to share the Gospel. If caught, they would immediately be put in prison. But that had not dissuaded them. "God is going to use us to go to the nations, and it may cost us our lives," they told me.

By 6:30 a.m. each day, they assembled in a small room. Together, they began to sing, lifting their praises to God in the predawn darkness. They stood, they kneeled, they cried, they sang, and they prayed with one primary theme: "Lord, send us to the lost of our nation. Lord, send us to the lost in all nations." Then, from 8 a.m. until 8 p.m., they sat on small plastic stools, eager to learn how to put that prayer into practice.

This is what comes to my mind when I picture bold faith. I believe this is the kind of faith Paul wrote about in 2 Corinthians 3:7-18, the passage we're studying this week. I wonder how we can experience the faith of those Asian missionaries here in the United States. I believe this passage may help our understanding of what true, bold, courageous faith looks like. Let's dive in and pray that God would use our time with Him this week to ignite this kind of faith in us.

Day 1 >

2 Corinthians 3:7-9;
Exodus 34:29-35

As we begin our last week of study on covenant, we're looking at a passage that brings together our study of the old covenant and new covenant. In order to understand 2 Corinthians 3:7-9, we need to read Exodus 34:29-35. These verses tell us about how the Israelites could not even look at Moses when he came down from his encounter with God because his face was shining so brightly.

Look at what Paul says in 2 Corinthians. The glory that was shining from Moses' face does not compare with the glory that shines through us because the Spirit of God is living in us! God's Spirit is dwelling in you and me at all times. Our lives should reflect His glory wherever we go.

Journal today about how your life is or is not reflecting God's glory. What might be keeping you from reflecting His glory? Pray that God would fill you with His Spirit so that His glory radiates through you.

Day 2 >>

2 Corinthians 3:10-11;
Jeremiah 31:31-34

Read 2 Corinthians 3:10-11. Here Paul contrasted the old covenant with the new covenant. To refresh your memory, go back

covenant: Knowing God—His Relationship with His People

and read Jeremiah 31:31-34, a passage which foretells the difference between the new covenant and the old covenant.

Now, get the picture of what Paul was saying in 2 Corinthians. It's kind of like when you look into the dark night sky and you see the moon shining. Its light is easily noticed in the dark sky. But when the sun rises in the morning, you can hardly even see the moon.

That's what the new covenant does to the old covenant. It shines so brightly that the new covenant is all we see. As you journal, reflect on all the differences between the old and the new covenants. Why does the new covenant shine brighter than the old covenant? Praise God today for establishing this new covenant with us that will shine forever.

Day 3 >>>
2 Corinthians 3:12-16; Isaiah 25:6-8

Paul continued to reference the covenant in the Old Testament. He talked about how the Israelites were not able to fully experience the glory of God. But things are different now. Jesus died on the cross and rose to life. Now we don't have anything separating us from the glory of God. We know Him completely because we've been forgiven for our sins.

This is what Isaiah is talking about in Isaiah 25:6-8. God, through Christ, has taken away the veil separating us from Him. One day, we will experience His glory in heaven with nothing keeping us from seeing all of His glory.

We don't have to hide when we enter the presence of God in prayer today, because Christ has taken care of all our sins. How does this truth affect your life today? How does this truth affect the way you pray? Journal today about other ways you can experience God's glory fully because of what Christ has done for you.

Day 4 >>>>>

2 Corinthians 3:17; Romans 8:1-4

A major difference between the old covenant and the new covenant is the Spirit of God. That's why Paul said in 2 Corinthians 3:17. In the old covenant, the people of God were unable to obey the Law completely. It only revealed their sinfulness and their condemnation before God.

But check out Romans 8:1-4. Because of the Spirit, there is no condemnation exists for those who trust in Jesus. The Spirit has set us free! Before we trusted in Christ, we were not able to obey the Law. But now that we have trusted in Christ for our salvation, the Spirit has set us free. We have the power to obey God.

Journal today about any struggles you are having. As you journal, think about how the Spirit has set you free from those struggles so that you have the power to obey God. Ask God to give you power and freedom by His Spirit today to obey Him completely.

Day 5 >>>>>
2 Corinthians 3:18; Romans 8:28-30

We have seen how we can experience God's glory because of Christ. Paul said we are being transformed into the likeness of Jesus more and more each day. That's the purpose of the Holy Spirit in us—to make us look more and more like Jesus.

Read Romans 8:28-30. God intends to make us more like Jesus. One day, those of us who have trusted in Christ and are being sanctified (being made to look more like Jesus) will be glorified. In other words, our transformation will be complete. We will live with Jesus in a place where no sin, no tears, and no pain exist forever.

Do you look more like Jesus today than you did yesterday? What can you do to look more like Jesus tomorrow than you do today. Pray that God would continually transform your life so that you experience His glory more and more in the covenant He has made with you.

A Final Word

Wow! We've spent a year studying what it means to be in covenant with God. To be honest, as we come to the end of this study, I am still amazed. I'm amazed God would reach down His hand to you and me and initiate a relationship with us. We grow accustomed to hearing the words, "God loves you." And many of us learned a song early in our lives . . . "Jesus loves me, this I know . . ." But we need to remember what an awesome truth this is. Even though we deserve eternal separation from God, He loves us and cares for us enough to enter into a covenant with us—a covenant that will l ast forever!

As we finish our study, I want to remind you of the four characteristics of covenant we laid out in the beginning of the year. First, covenant is all about a relationship with God. The passages we've studied this year are not just words on a page; they represent a relationship we have with the God of the universe! Second, covenant is all about God's unchanging promises. We don't need to fear anything in life or in death because we know our covenant with God is based on eternal promises. Third, covenant is all about God's grace. He is the One who initiates a relationship with us and changes our hearts so that we enjoy

the blessings of knowing and following Him. And finally, covenant is all about faith. Faith is believing that what God said in His Word is true and then letting His truth direct every part of our lives.

We've studied Scripture from Genesis to Revelation this year, and now, believing that all we've studied is true, we're ready to experience the incredible joy of trusting God with our families, our friendships, our plans, our dreams, and our futures. And when we trust Him, we know that God will definitely show Himself to be trustworthy. That's what covenant is all about!

covenant: Knowing God—His Relationship with His People